COLD BLOODED

This is a true story, represented here as factually as possible. In order to maintain their anonymity, in some instances I have changed the names of individuals and places. I may have changed some identifying characteristics and details, such as physical properties, occupations, and places of residence.

Photos used with permission from *Fort Smith Times Record, Van Buren Press Argus-Courier*, Mary Jane Mustard, Joan Sloat, and from the murder-trial transcript of Thomas W. Simmons.

ISBN: 978-1-68313-204-2
LCCN: 2019936014

Cover and interior design by Kelsey Rice

First Edition

Printed and bound in the USA

COLD BLOODED

A CHILLING TRUE TALE OF TERROR, RAPE, AND MURDER IN THE ARKANSAS RIVER BOTTOMS

by ANITA PADDOCK

AUTHOR OF *BLIND RAGE*

P

Pen-L Publishing

Fayetteville, Arkansas

Pen-L.com

BOOKS BY ANITA PADDOCK

Blind Rage

Closing Time

Cold Blooded

DEDICATION

For my children, David X Williams and Jennifer Leslie Paddock

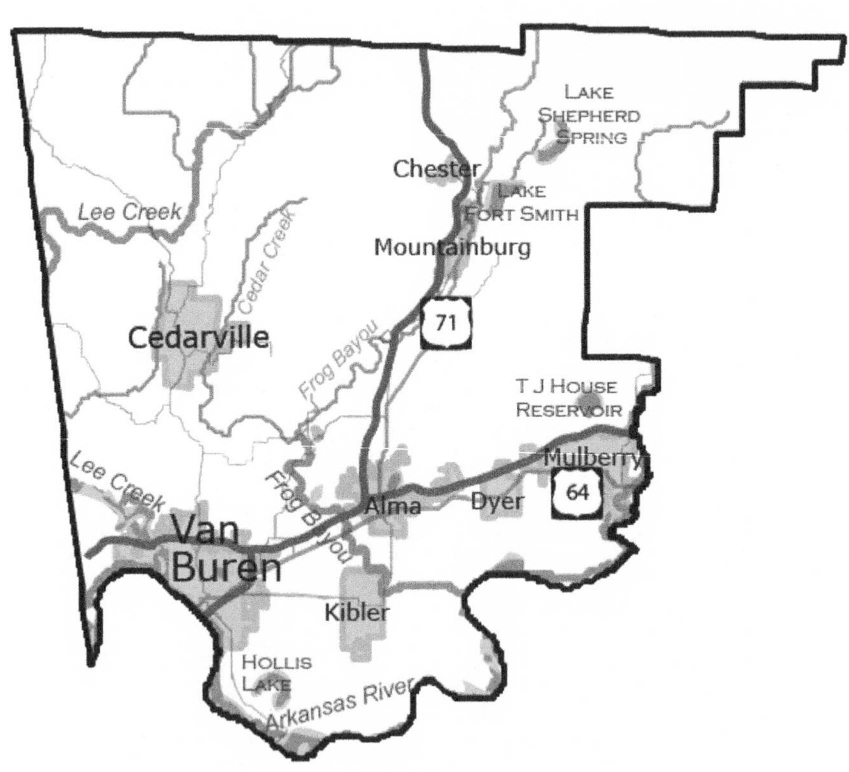

Map of Crawford County

SUPREME COURT OF ARKANSAS OPINION FEBRUARY 7, 1983

In comparing this death sentence with similar cases, as is our practice, we know of no other case involving multiple murders as cold blooded, so brutal, so lacking in any trace of humanity as those committed by this person.

CHAPTER ONE

Jawana Price was feeling the blues on that cold January morning in 1981. Christmas was over. So was New Year's Day. Nursing school hadn't started again after the Christmas vacation that had begun with anticipation and excitement. Today was the fifth of January, which meant five more days until Jawana could leave her part-time secretarial job at Phoenix Village Mall and get back to the books and her classmates and actually having contact with patients. She was in her last semester of nursing at Westark, Fort Smith's community college not far from where they lived. Ever since she was a little girl, she'd dreamed of becoming a nurse.

She looked around her apartment's one bedroom, proud of her new bedspread she'd gotten for Christmas. Larry said it was a little girlish for his taste, but if she liked it, it was okay with him. Her Siamese cat liked it also. In fact, Jawana had shooed her off it so many times that she had finally given up and just let her beloved cat sleep wherever she wanted. Jawana also loved her small aquarium with a few guppies and goldfish. She especially loved her husband.

She picked up the silver frame that held their wedding picture taken in August of 1978. Larry had on his glasses, and she wished she had asked him to take them off before the photographer took the picture. She was saving for him to get contacts. He didn't know it though. It was going to be a surprise.

Jawana was eager to get back to school, where she would begin her nursing rotations in Pediatrics, Psychology, and ICU. She smiled, feeling elated over what she, a little country girl from Flat Rock, Arkansas, had accomplished. She came from an even smaller community than Larry. Lamar was big compared to Flat Rock.

They had met in Lamar High School and dated from the twelfth grade on. Everybody said they were a cute couple, and she guessed they were. They had fun together, still did. She was shy, but Larry wasn't. She was short and he was tall. They were both brunettes with thick hair. They'd make pretty babies.

She placed the picture back on the dresser and pulled out her underwear and pantyhose and began dressing for the day. Larry was out for a test drive with a man who had answered an ad Larry had placed in the *Southwest Times Record* to sell a 1979 silver and maroon Ford LTD. The car belonged to Holly Gentry, their friend who was part owner in the complex, Glenn-Holly, where they lived, and which they now managed. Holly was a neat guy. A good Christian who had befriended them almost as soon as he gave them the key to their first apartment in Fort Smith. She thanked God every day for his friendship.

She and Larry talked so much about Holly over Christmas that her daddy said he wanted to meet this man with a girl's name.

Jawana took a pair of khaki slacks and brown shoes from her closet and a white top from the middle dresser drawer she and Larry shared and continued dressing. She knew her husband and the man had returned because she could hear them talking in the living room. She hoped the man liked the car. She wished she and Larry could afford to buy it.

One of their neighbors had told them that a man had come by on Saturday afternoon to look at the car. "To tell you the truth, he didn't look like he could afford that car," he'd told Larry. But Larry just laughed and said, "Don't judge a book by its cover."

The ad had been in the paper since the sixteenth of December, and it was scheduled to end on the sixth of January. Larry didn't want to have to mess with placing another ad and going through all the no-shows again.

Jawana turned on the clock radio they kept on a little wicker shelf above the commode. KISR was playing "Nine to Five," a song she liked. She glanced at her Timex watch and knew, right after this song, Fred Baker would give the weather. He always made things as dramatic as possible, whether it was a violent tornado coming, a raging flood, or a crippling ice storm.

KISR was a popular music station, with a morning listening audience said to be twenty thousand in the mornings and eighteen thousand in the afternoons. Everybody Jawana knew listened to KISR.

"Cloudy and cold today, with winds out of the northwest. High in the low forties. Better bundle up those kiddos heading back to school in Mountainburg, Rudy, Kibler, Chester, Figure Five, Cedarville, Sunset Corners, Pocola, and all areas in-between."

She chuckled at Fred Baker naming all the little towns on either side of the Arkansas River that separated Arkansas from Oklahoma. She switched off the radio, grabbed her heavy brown sweater off the chair where she'd tossed it the night before, and opened the bedroom door.

"Good morning," she said. Larry was wearing his blue plaid shirt she'd given him for Christmas. His blue eyes really sparkled when he wore blue. "So how was the test drive?" Jawana asked.

Larry stood up from where he was sitting on the living room couch. He walked over and put his arm around his wife.

"This nice guy wants to buy the car."

Jawana smiled at the man and told him hello. She noticed that Larry had made coffee because two cups sat on their coffee table. That was just like Larry. He never met a stranger, and here he was sitting in their apartment drinking coffee with a man he'd only met thirty minutes earlier.

The man nodded and offered half a smile. "Nice to meet you."

Jawana thought the man looked a little scary. His blue jacket was frayed around the collar and sleeves, and under it, he wore a blue shirt with what looked like an insulated shirt under it. He had a mustache and long curly sideburns, and he swooped his brown hair over to one side to hide his growing baldness. His glasses were odd-looking, out of fashion, with thick lens and black frames. He was thin, with a sunken-looking chest, but he looked tough. And she detected a body odor. She didn't see how in the world he could come up with over four thousand dollars to buy the car. But she'd let Larry worry about that.

She grabbed her purse off the kitchen counter and pulled on her brown sweater. She smiled at Larry and said, "I'll see you for lunch then around noon?"

Her husband kissed her cheek. "Want to try some Mexican?"

"Sounds good." And then Jawana added, "Fred Baker says it's going to be cold today, so you better wear that heavy windbreaker."

Neither Jawana nor Larry liked to wear coats. They felt constricted in them, especially while driving. They seemed to agree on nearly everything.

Jawana opened the front door and checked her watch that read eight forty. "I'll see you about noon then."

Larry said, "I'll walk you to the car."

"And will you feed the cat and the fish?"

"Sure thing," Larry said. Then he turned to the man and said, "I have to do all the hard work around here."

Larry Price thought it odd that the guy didn't laugh at his joke. His only response was a cold, hard stare. Then he asked Larry if he could use the phone.

"I need to call my wife and tell her about the car. I'm buying it for her."

Larry wanted to sell the car, so he said, "Sure, it's in the bedroom. I'll be right back."

Larry held Jawana's hand as they walked to her car. She took her keys out of her purse and handed them to him, which was a ritual they usually followed each morning.

He unlocked the door and held it for her while she slid under the wheel. Then he gave her back the keys, and she started it up and let the motor run for a few minutes.

"I don't like you leaving that man in our house alone."

"Don't worry, honey. I'll see you at noon." With that, Larry Price turned around and ran back inside his apartment.

Thomas Simmons hadn't counted on meeting Larry Price's wife. When he knocked on the door that morning to inquire about the car, he was hoping to only talk to Larry. His plan was to ask for a test drive, dump Price off somewhere out in the country, and turn the car over to his buddy in Van Buren, who was going to buy it from him. John Dickerson specialized in stolen cars, and he'd already promised Tom fifteen hundred dollars cash if he delivered it to him on Monday afternoon. Tom supposed it was wishful thinking for him to assume that his plans would go like clockwork.

While Larry walked his wife to her car, Tom snooped around the bedroom. He found a checkbook in a drawer of the dresser, tore out the top check, and returned the checkbook where he found it. He sat down on the living room couch just as Larry walked back inside.

"My wife said she wanted to see the car," Simmons said. "Would you mind if I drove it over to show her? She works at Central Mall, and I could run it over there right quick."

"Gee, Mr. Simmons, I wouldn't feel right letting you drive the car without me. It's not that I don't trust you, but the car doesn't really belong to me. I'm just selling it for a friend, so I feel responsible."

Simmons felt a little unsure of what he should say next. He fought to control his anger.

"Guess I shouldn't have asked. All my life, I've had to beg someone to trust me."

"I'll be glad to ride with you, though. I've got nowhere to be until noon when I pick up Jawana at Phoenix Village where she works. We're having Mexican for lunch. Then I'll have to be at work at three."

"Where you work?"

"Baldor. I'm a machinist."

"That a good job?"

Larry Price smiled. "Oh, man, it's a great place to work. I've been there for over a year now."

"I'm going to Westark. I want to get into computers. That's the coming thing, you know. I've got a bit of a natural talent for it," Simmons said. He was feeling confident that he could talk this Mr. Nice Guy Price back inside the LTD.

"Well, you want to show the car to your wife?"

"Yeah, you drive. That way it won't be my fault if we get into a wreck on the way to the mall."

Larry Price laughed. "I'll be happy to let you drive."

Thomas Simmons shook his head. "Nope. You've already told me in so many words that you don't trust me." He clutched the pistol he was carrying in his jacket pocket, pulled it out.

"Come on. Let's take that ride."

Larry Price's face went white. His hands shook as he raised them.

"Go ahead. Take the car."

"Nope. You are going to walk out to the car and get in the driver's seat. Don't try to get away. All I really wanted was the car. It's gone too far now. I got to take you with me."

CHAPTER TWO

Jawana drove her little two-door orange Maverick west down Grand Avenue where traffic was heavy with mothers returning from taking their kids to school and other workers who had to be at work at nine o'clock. She put her left blinkers on and turned south on Greenwood Avenue, past Sally Ann's and on the other side of the street LeJon's Gifts, Dorothy's Dress Shop, and Vivian's Book Store. Around the corner on Park was The Corner House that served the best sandwiches and salads in town. All the Northside High School kids could walk there on their lunch hour. Jawana and her friends from school tried to go there at least once a month, especially after big tests.

She turned west again on Rogers, past the Immaculate Catholic Church at the Y, and turned south on Towson Avenue with its pawn shops and used car lots. Seven minutes later, she parked at the Phoenix Village Shopping Mall's entrance where the business offices were.

She stayed in her car an extra five minutes, listening to the trucks whizzing behind her on Wheeler Avenue. She sure did hope she could shake this funny feeling she was having. After looking up depression in one of her textbooks, she decided it might have something to do with her periods or the anxiety she felt about her last semester of school and graduation.

She opened the door and locked her little car. She put on her biggest smile and tucked her head against the cold wind that whistled across the parking lot to the offices of Mr. Jewel Morris and Mr. Howard Gentry, who co-owned the mall. Her day began at nine, and she was five minutes early. She liked everybody she worked with, including the owners, whom she admired greatly. They were both country boys who'd worked hard all their lives and now owned this beautiful mall.

Mr. Jewel Morris, Jr. was the son of school teachers Jewel and Nita Morris, who'd taught in little country schools all around Crawford County, across the Arkansas River from Fort Smith, which was in Sebastian County where she and Larry lived.

Mr. Morris had grown up in a little community called Kibler and gone to high school in Alma, a little town east of there. He went to college at Fort Smith Junior College, which became Westark Community College, and got into the NROTC program shortly before Pearl Harbor. From there, the Navy sent him to other colleges, where he ended up at Harvard University. "Pretty good for a country boy from Kibler, Arkansas," he liked to tell people. "I didn't have one bit of trouble keeping up with that Harvard bunch."

Mr. Howard Gentry was also born in the Kibler area. In fact, the elder Mr. Morris had been one of his school teachers. Mr. Gentry worked in the oil business in Arkansas, Oklahoma, Louisiana, and ended his oil business career in Venezuela. Always a hard worker, he saved his money and eventually returned to Crawford County and built a ranch around Cedarville, another little town north of Van Buren, which was the county seat of Crawford County. He then got into real estate construction that led to the first shopping mall in the state of Arkansas

Jawana knew that both men were devout Christians and practiced their faith daily. The Lord had definitely smiled down on them. She and Larry often talked about the two men who'd both been born in little Kibler.

"We'll have to take a drive down there some Sunday after church," Larry often said. "You know, just to see what it's like, with all its beautiful farmland."

Jawana walked down the long hallway to the offices and opened the door.

"Good morning, everybody," she said. "You guys ready for me to make the coffee?"

Like always, Holly Gentry was the first to speak. He was always quick to tell the cute little things his boy, Jeremy, who was five, had done. He was the carbon copy of Holly. Jeremy liked to go fishing with his daddy and ride horses on the ranch his granddaddy owned. His little sister, Robyn, was just a year old, and she looked and acted like her mama, Debbie. Their children called Jewel Morris "Uncle Jewel," even though he wasn't their uncle. It was a nickname of love.

While Jawana waited for the coffee to perk, she listened to Holly talk about his son, and she hoped she and Larry would one day have a family as sweet and nice as Holly's.

Holly took the cup of coffee Jawana poured for him.

"Are you anxious for school to start?" he asked.

"You know I am. I'm afraid my brain has turned to mush."

"I doubt that," Holly said while stirring a healthy spoonful of sugar in his coffee. "You're the best secretary we've ever had, and I know you'll be a fantastic nurse, the best to ever graduate from Westark. We're all real proud of you, girl."

Jawana could feel her face blush. She hadn't yet learned how to accept a compliment without being a little embarrassed, so she changed the subject.

"Holly, you'd better get on down to your store. Who knows how many folks will come in today to buy a Razorback shirt?"

Holly's store was named "Sooieville" in honor of the cheer Arkansas fans yelled for their Razorbacks: Woo Pig Sooie. He flashed his million-dollar smile that had won over men and women since he was five years old.

"Eddie Sutton will win the Southwest Conference this year," Holly said. "With Scott Hastings and U.S. Reed playing like they are, I'm really pumped. I've got a friend who has season tickets, and he and I have split the cost. Debbie thinks I'm crazy, but man, oh man, I love the way these guys play defense."

"How 'bout them hogs?" Mr. Howard Gentry called out as he walked down the hall, just outside the office.

Holly answered with a "Woo pig sooie!"

Jawana laughed. It seemed the whole state of Arkansas was obsessed with sports.

Lou Holtz had been the football coach for four years, and the fans weren't happy over his performance, but Eddie Sutton was like a king. Fans went wild over Sutton.

Holly had graduated from the U of A and had played college baseball at Westark. He was downright crazy over sports. In fact, Jawana thought, Holly Gentry was downright crazy with life. She bet he'd never felt depressed for one day.

"Oh yeah, Holly, I almost forgot to tell you. Larry had a guy come by and look at your car this morning. He thinks he has it sold."

Holly smiled and pumped his fist in the air. "That's great. This new year is starting off just fine. Yes-siree Bob, just fine and dandy."

CHAPTER THREE

Holly Kim Gentry felt optimistic about the new year. His plans for building a strip mall were on target. He and his big brother, Mark, who was a minister and taught at Central Bible College in Springfield, Missouri, felt called to build the stores to finance Mark's mission work. They were both devoted to their church, Faith Assembly of God in Fort Smith, and it was through Holly's work with the youth of his church that he had seen the need to carry the gospel to young children in other parts of the world.

He led a group of boys called The Royal Rangers, and he took them hiking and camping at his dad's place, White River Ranch. The year before he'd taken them to the Rockies to camp out.

Holly had often been asked where he got his name.

"My sweet mama, Odessa Howard, loved cowboys," was his standard reply. "She saw a movie with Jimmy Stewart, and he played the hero whose name was Holly."

Howard and Odessa often took their two boys and one girl to the drive-in movies to see Westerns starring James Stewart, Gary Cooper, and John Wayne. Because the family owned a ranch with horses and cattle, it was only natural that Westerns were their favorite.

Mark was also an accomplished pilot and owned a Mooney Executive 21 with all the instruments available. Both his mother and his father were pilots. The ranch had an airstrip, and Mark frequently flew from Springfield to the ranch.

Over the past Christmas, the family had been all together for the holiday. The two brothers stood outside on the patio, away from the usual family noises of kids playing with their new toys and the television blaring with football games.

It was cold, but both brothers were warmly dressed in suede jackets and felt cowboy hats. They stood without speaking, enjoying the quiet and comfort of being with each other. Soon, though, they began talking about the situation in Tehran, Iran, where sixty had been taken hostage at the American Embassy. There was anti-American sentiment, led by the followers of Khomeini who were angry because the United States had allowed the deposed Shah of Iran to come there for cancer treatment. President Carter had attempted a rescue, but it failed because of a sand storm and Americans were killed. Carter had lost the election, and Ronald Reagan had won and would take office in January.

"I'd fight as hard as I could," Holly said, changing the subject of many being captured to one in a kidnapping or carjacking. "Nobody would take me alive."

Mark agreed. "If you go with a kidnapper, you're as good as dead." He had spent years in the Crawford County Sheriff's Mounted Patrol, founded by then-sheriff, Bill Vickery. "I've had so much training over the years with FBI courses and spending time overseas that I know the rule is 'Never Be Taken Alive.' Make them kill you where they've grabbed you."

The brothers continued with their talk, each espousing the other's bravery and top-notch physical condition. Although Mark was taller and played sports, Holly was the better athlete. He'd played short-stop in college before transferring to the university at Fayetteville. Everyone said he was "a great little athlete."

As the sun slid from the horizon in rays of pinks and golds, Mark reached his arm over his brother's back. "Sunsets are the prettiest in the winter, I think."

Holly agreed. "Who could not believe in our creator?" he asked while tears filled his eyes. "We're lucky, Mark. Jesus loves us, and He knows we love him. His grace has covered us with his blessings."

"Amen."

Neither brother knew that they would never again watch another winter sunset together at their father's ranch.

CHAPTER FOUR

On Monday morning, the fifth of January, Jim Pence—the foreman of the Jenny Lind quarry, owned by Arkhola Sand and Gravel Company—was notified that Thomas Simmons would not be at work that day. It was the first day the plant had reopened since they'd shut down for Christmas.

Pence sat in his chair, already working at his desk. He looked up. "What was his reason?"

His secretary raised her eyebrows, hinting at her skepticism. "He said he had a car wreck and wouldn't be in until Tuesday."

Pence lit his second cigarette of the morning. "Was he hurt?"

"Guess not."

Pence didn't want to have to replace Simmons. He was proving to be a good employee, and he was one of the hardest workers he'd ever had at the job of shovel boy. Simmons had only been employed since Thanksgiving, and he already had a reputation for being tough. Once when he was cleaning out from under the primary crusher, a large rock fell off and hit him in the back, causing him to fall to the ground. He just got up, put his hard hat back on, and kept working like nothing had happened.

Jim Pence smiled, remembering the recent Christmas party the company had held at the Holiday Inn in Fort Smith. He had found himself standing next to Bill Scarbrough, the personnel manager of Arkhola.

"How's the new guy working out?" Scarbrough had asked.

"Tough as nails," Pence replied and regaled Scarbrough with the story of the shovel boy getting up immediately after a boulder fell on his back. "Any other guy would be in shock. The other men couldn't believe it. They said he hopped up like nothing had happened. A lesser man wouldn't have been able to stand up for days."

Scarbrough had laughed loudly, causing his wife, Pam, to wonder if he'd had a little too much eggnog. "You know I called the employment office looking for someone to work that shitty job. It's a hard job, man, and it's hard for me to find someone to work it."

Pence had nodded and said, "Yeah, they come and go pretty fast."

"Well, the employment office routed me to a federal probation officer who was looking for a job for his guy who'd just gotten out of prison."

"Yeah, he knew you were desperate."

"The probation officer told me about Simmons. He'd been paroled and was staying with his sister in Kibler. He needed to find him a job."

"So?" Pence asked. "I guess you needed a guy and there wasn't nobody else. It's a SLJ, for sure"

Bill laughed. "Yep, it's a shitty little job, no two ways about it. The federal guy knew it too," he said, slapping Pence on the back. "I'm glad it's working out for you. I guess everyone deserves a second chance."

"I've been taking him down to the Jenny Lind Store and having him try out one of those tuna fish sandwiches everybody loves so much. He works so damn hard. I tell him he needs to take a break, smoke a cigarette every once in a while. We've had some heart-to-heart talks, and I like the guy. He deserves a chance to change his life. His sister thought so too, I guess. Simmons told me he'd fried fish for his sister and her boyfriend at a fish fry up at Lake Fort Smith."

The word *fish* caused the subject to quickly change. Just the word set off a yearning each man had to once again be fishing in a boat on a lazy summer afternoon. Then they walked over to a table covered with a green cloth and decorated with red poinsettias. They sat down with their wives and enjoyed their meal of prime rib. Each asked for another cup of eggnog. They exchanged fishing stories. Some were even true.

In Greenwood, Arkansas, a little town south of Fort Smith, Ray Tate crawled out of bed on Monday, January fifth. He patted his belly, reassuring himself that the diet he'd started immediately after Christmas was helping him shed the pounds he'd gained over the holiday. He was thirty-three years old and weighed one eighty.

He had the red-brick house to himself. His wife, Anita Ruth, and their kids, Tony and Christina, had already left for work and school. He had a good marriage. They had been high school sweethearts in Siloam Springs. Their relatives still lived there, and they visited often.

Tate had a weight limit he had to follow with the Fort Smith Police Department, where he was a detective. He was also a master sergeant with the Arkansas Air National Guard Reserves as a recruiter.

With reddish-brown hair and a smattering of freckles, Tate was the obvious target of redhead jokes. He was a likable guy and didn't mind the teasing. In fact, he gave as good as he got.

Work started at three that afternoon, and he dressed in a white shirt, blue tie, gray trousers and sport coat, and black boots. His pistol, handcuffs, and badge were in place on his belt. He grabbed his cigarettes and a ball point pen and pencil set from the top of his dresser and placed them in his shirt pocket. After tucking his compact New Testament Bible and a small red notebook in the pocket of his tan overcoat, he grabbed his keys and headed out the door.

His third cigarette of the day, Vantage brand, was already between his lips as he traveled down Highway 10 toward the Fort Smith Police Department. He always enjoyed his drive to work on this stretch of the road. There were few businesses and only a few homes dotted the countryside. Although the landscape was mostly a burnished gold with winter's dormancy, an occasional cedar tree added color. And on fence rows lining the highway, shrubs with bright-red berries looked like Christmas lights. He made a note to himself to go by the Fort Smith Public Library that was near the police station. He'd ask one of the nice ladies who worked there what the name of those berries was. If they didn't know, they would soon find out. He thought it would be great to work in a place where all you had to do to find answers to questions was open a book.

He drove a few more miles, when suddenly he hit his palm on the steering wheel. "Damn," he said. He'd have to turn around and go back home. He'd forgotten his flashlight.

CHAPTER FIVE

Simmons leaned his back against the front door, with his left leg bent at the knee on the seat. He was uncomfortable in that position, but it was the only way he could safely keep his eye on the driver.

They were driving on the old highway between Van Buren and Alma, a route that Simmons thought would be less crowded.

"Just keep it slow," he said. "Don't get over fifty."

"What are you going to do?" Larry Price asked for the tenth time. "Please don't kill me."

"I ain't going to kill you. Damn it straight to hell, keep quiet and let me think."

They drove down Highway 64-71 until they came to Shibley Road.

"Turn here to the right."

They stayed on the road, which was paved but rife with holes, big and small and full of muddy water.

"Where are you taking me?" Larry asked. "Where are we? I'm not familiar with the country around here."

"Just keep driving. We'll turn at the next crossroads."

After ten more minutes of driving, Simmons directed Larry to turn into an area marked with a sign that read Clear Creek Park. Larry saw that the park was deserted, which made his heart sink.

"You don't have a clue where you are, do you? Simmons asked. "You see the river, don't you? I could shoot you and throw you into the damn river. Maybe a duck hunter will see your body. But I'm not. I'm just going to leave you here. You can get back however the hell you can."

"Why are you doing this? You're going to kill me so you can have this car? That's insane. Why kill someone over a car?"

"Jesus, man, shut the fuck up. I said I wasn't going to kill you. Stop here at this picnic table."

Larry turned off the ignition. He left both hands on the wheel, and he refused to get out of the car when Simmons told him to.

He rammed the pistol into his side. "Get out," I said. "Sit down at that table."

Larry did as he was told.

"Hold your hands out."

With a heavy cord he carried in his pants pocket, he tied Larry's wrists together. Tight.

"Now start walking that way toward the trees." Simmons followed. "I'm not going to kill you. I'm just going to leave you here. You'll be able to see your cute little wife again."

He reached for the collar of Larry's jacket, he pulled it up over his neck and halfway up his head, placed the pistol against the cloth, and fired one shot into the back of Larry's head.

Then he walked back to the stolen car, wiped off all fingerprints, and drove toward Industrial Park Road to a Citizens Bank. After setting the stage to throw off law enforcement, he went inside and deposited a forged check for three hundred fifty dollars signed by Larry.

"I'd like to have two twenties and a ten back in cash."

CHAPTER SIX

Jawana Price stood inside the entrance of Phoenix Village Mall at noon January 5th, waiting for her husband. She was hungry, and she'd been thinking about a burrito smothered in cheese and red sauce. Larry teased her because she never ordered anything but a burrito—just one, never two.

She looked at her Timex watch, realizing Larry was close to twenty minutes late. It worried her, and she began to fear he'd had a wreck or had suddenly gotten sick. She stepped outside into the cold wind and looked all around the parking lot, hoping she'd see him. *Oh, Larry, honey, come on. I'm hungry.*

At twelve forty-five, she gave up and went back into the office, where Holly was finishing a sandwich he'd brought from home. He always left his shop at noon, so he could eat with his daddy, but today his dad and his partner, Jewel Morris, had gone to Rotary Club.

"You already back?" he said, looking at his Seiko watch.

"No, Larry didn't pick me up. I'm worried sick. I'm going to call my neighbor to go check on him." With that, she picked up the phone and dialed the number of her friend, Carol Gilbert, who lived in the same apartment complex.

"Hi, this is Jawana." She knew Carol worked nights and that she was probably just getting up. "I'm sorry to ask you, but do you mind walking down and see if Larry's home? He was supposed to pick me up for lunch, and I'm worried. And see if that car we had for sale is still parked out front."

Jawana gave the office number to her friend and hung up. Tears began to fill her eyes, and she reached for the Kleenex she kept in the top drawer of her desk.

When the phone rang, Jawana jumped, but she picked it up before the second ring. "Yes, Carol?"

"I called and got no answer, and then I went down and knocked on the door. A bunch of times. Your cat peeked around the curtains on the front window and just about scared me to death."

"What about Larry's car? Was it there?" Larry always parked in a certain spot, and that's where it was when she'd left him earlier that morning. When she left him with the man who was looking at the car. *Oh Lord, that guy was pretty rough-looking.*

"Yes, Jawana. Larry's car is definitely there, but the car he was selling is gone."

"Oh Lord, Carol, I'm really worried. This is not like Larry."

She said goodbye to Carol and tried to think where he could have gone and if he would have driven the LTD if something had happened to his car.

"I'm going to call Larry's parents in Lamar. Maybe something happened at home. It's long distance, Holly, but I'll pay for it."

"Don't be silly, Jawana," Holly said. "Call whoever you need to call."

She placed the call to Larry's parents first. She tried to hide the alarm in her voice, but when her mother-in-law answered, her voice broke.

"I'm sorry to call you, but have you all talked to Larry? He was supposed to pick me up for lunch, but he didn't come or call me at work. I'm just worried, and I thought you or his dad might be sick."

When told they hadn't heard from their son, Jawana began to cry.

"I'm sorry," she said, "but it's not like Larry to not pick me up when he's supposed to."

Mrs. Price asked Jawana if she'd called Baldor, where Larry worked.

"You know, they might have called him to come in early, and he didn't have a chance to call you. I'm sure he's okay. You call his work."

Jawana wasn't sure if she should call Larry at work. A big company like that probably didn't like wives calling up and asking if their husband was there.

"What do you think, Holly? Should I call his work?"

Holly was already looking up the phone number for Baldor in the phone book.

"Baldor's got a wonderful reputation for taking care of their employees," he said. "Larry works in the department that works on endplates, correct?"

"Yeah, he's a machinist."

Holly jotted down the number on a pad and handed it to Jawana.

"You call right now," he said. "We need to put your mind at ease."

A woman who worked in the office told Jawana that a man had called earlier and said that Larry Price wouldn't be at work.

"I asked him if Mr. Price would be in on the next day, but he told me he didn't know," the lady at the desk said.

That chilled Jawana to her core. *Who would have called and said that about Larry?* Something was definitely wrong.

Then Jawana did what any young woman scared to death would do, if she had the chance. She called her mama and daddy, Mr. and Mrs. Claude Parker of Flat Rock, Arkansas. Maybe her little brother, Ronnie, had gotten into some kind of trouble at school, and he'd called Larry for help. But Ronnie was the best kid she knew, and he never got in trouble anywhere, anytime.

When her mother answered the phone, Jawana could hear the television playing in the living room. She knew her mom was watching her favorite soap opera, *As the World Turns.*

But like her mother-in-law, Jawana's mom had not heard from Larry.

"Now try not to worry. Larry's okay, I'm sure of it. He just let the time get away from him, and maybe he had car trouble and he had to get a ride with a friend. You never know about these guys."

Jawana felt a little better, talking to her mother.

Then her mom chuckled.

"Why, your daddy has made me worry for no good reason lots of times. I'm sure everything is just fine. Yes, I'm sure of it. Everything will be just fine. You'll see, daughter."

Holly Gentry was a handsome guy everyone wanted as their friend. He smiled all the time, loved his Lord, loved his wife, loved his kids. Athletic and ambitious. Few people could find a single fault in Holly. Maybe his mama knew something, but she wasn't talking.

"Let me drive over to the apartments, Jawana," Holly said. "I'd feel better to see for myself."

He walked to the front of the mall, the side that faced Towson Avenue, and climbed into his brown four-wheel-drive Ford truck. He was as worried as Jawana was, but he tried not to show it. He said his prayers on the way to the apartments, but when he got there, Larry's old Ford Galaxy was still parked in his usual spot. The LTD was gone, as the neighbor had said.

Puzzled for sure, and now a little frightened, Holly walked over to the Price apartment and knocked several times. Jawana's Siamese cat poked its head out between the curtains and looked at him, and then, just as quick, exited the window.

Holly walked down to the mailboxes to see if Larry had left a note there, but he saw nothing. In fact, he didn't think the mail had even been delivered yet.

Discouraged, he drove back to Phoenix Village Mall.

In Lamar, the Price family worried.

In Flat Rock, the Parker family fretted.

After Holly returned to the offices at Phoenix Village, he made up his mind that his friend's disappearance was beyond troubling. It was downright scary, and he resolved to tell Jawana that they should go and talk to the police. Not only was his friend missing, but the LTD that was worth close to five thousand dollars was missing also.

He checked in at his store, Sooieville, to see if he needed to stay there with his employee who'd come in at noon. But business was slow, so he went on to the office. There he found his dad, Howard, and Jewel Morris, the other owner of the mall, who had returned from their luncheon meeting. Jewel Morris was his dad's best friend, and together they were trying to make Phoenix Village Mall into a viable business operation. There had been some low periods, but neither man was willing to throw in the towel.

They were doing their best to console Jawana, but their furrowed brows and restless bodies told Holly that the whole bunch of them were approaching a near panic mode.

Mr. Morris said he'd go down to the police station, but Holly insisted he should be the one to go.

"I'm the one who asked Larry to sell my car," Holly said. "It's only right that I go with her.

"It's getting cold out there, Jawana. Get your coat and let's go down to the police station. It's settled. Everyone thinks we should, so let's go. The quicker we act, the better off Larry will be."

Jawana grabbed her brown sweater and pulled it on, buttoning the wooden buttons.

"Lord, girl," Holly said. "Don't you have a coat?"

“This is all I’ve got,” she said. “I’m not used to wearing coats. I’ll be okay.”

“Well, I’m wearing mine. Let me get it out of Dad’s office, and we’ll get going.”

When he returned, he had his overcoat on.

“Well, at least one of us will be warm,” Holly said. He was trying to ease the tension in the room, but it was impossible. Larry Price was missing. So was the car. Something had happened. Something very terrible had happened. He was certain of it.

“Should I take my car?” Jawana asked.

“No, we’ll go in my truck. It’s already warm. Let’s go.”

CHAPTER SEVEN

The Fort Smith Police Station was on South Tenth, ten blocks off Garrison Avenue, which ended at the bridge that crossed the Arkansas River into Oklahoma. Moffett, Oklahoma, was a rough little spot that sat almost under the bridge, along the river banks. During World War II, the Army soldiers stationed at Camp Chaffee in Barling, Arkansas, were barred from going to Moffett, where beer joints that promoted gambling and prostitution thrived.

Fertile river bottoms could also be seen from the bridge, where soybeans, corn, spinach, wheat, tomatoes, and watermelons grew. The "bottoms," whether on the Arkansas side or the Oklahoma side, were where farmers made or lost a fortune, mainly because of the weather. The bottoms were also places where nobody but farmers and their families needed to be.

Actions by unsavory people sometimes occurred down in the bottoms, not the least of which involved sexual activities, spurred by alcoholic beverages. Often times, high school boys were warned by their parents: "Don't you dare go down in those river bottoms at night. You can duck hunt there during the day, but that's all."

Neither Jawana nor Holly was thinking about the river bottoms when they parked in front of the police station. They were directed to an office where Detective Ray Tate and Detective James "Poncho" Davis listened as they explained the situation.

Jawana spoke first. "My husband, Larry Price, was supposed to pick me up today at the Phoenix Village Mall where I work. We made plans for noon. We meet for lunch a lot, especially when I don't have class. I'm in nursing school at Westark, but during Christmas break I work as a secretary for Holly and his family."

Jawana paused, waiting for the detectives to lay down their pens.

"I start classes next Monday, so this was going to be our last day to have lunch together before school started. He works the three to eleven shift, so we really never have supper together."

Detective Tate was the first to speak. "How old is Larry?"

Jawana's voice broke, but she was able to answer. "We're both twenty-one."

"Where does Larry work?"

"Baldor. He's a machinist. I've already called there, but the secretary or someone told me a man, not Larry, had called and said he wouldn't be in for work that day."

"We're so concerned, detectives, because Larry was selling a car for me, an LTD Ford," Holly said. "A sharp-looking 1978 model, maroon with a gray top."

"And a man came to look at it this morning just as I was headed to work," Jawana added.

Ray Tate was thinking all along that this Price guy maybe had a girlfriend, but when Jawana mentioned the man who came about the car, his pulse quickened. He felt the hairs on the back of his neck rise.

"What did this guy look like?"

Jawana gave a description the best she could remember. "He was in his forties. Skinny. Thinning brown hair. Sideburns. Wore glasses and had a mustache. He seemed dirty to me."

"What else do you remember, Mrs. Price?" asked Tate.

"He said the car was for his wife, and he asked to use our phone to call her about the car."

Holly said, "Larry's car is at the apartment, but the LTD is gone. I went there to check, but Larry's not there."

"And the time you last saw your husband?"

Tears slid down Jawana's face, which she wiped with her sleeve. "About eight forty this morning."

She was desperately afraid she'd never see her husband again. She'd be lost without him. She sobbed quietly, covering her face with both hands. The three men in the room were powerless to help her.

Holly felt like crying too. "This is all my fault," he said. "I asked Larry to sell the car."

Poncho Davis cleared his throat and reminded everyone in the room that the police would get to work and find Larry Price.

"Maybe this guy let Larry out on some back road and has taken the car to California. Who knows? Do you happen to have the papers on the car with you, Mr. Gentry? We'll get an APB out on it soon as we have the license plate and VIN number."

"All that paperwork is at our apartment," Jawana said. "I know right where it is."

Ray Tate couldn't help but think about his wife and how frightened she would be if he went missing.

"Let's finish up this report," Tate said, "and then we'll go over to your apartment."

Poncho looked at his watch. He remembered he had a meeting at six o'clock at Belle Grove that he couldn't miss.

"Ray, you go with them to the apartment and get back to me here around seven. Okay?"

"Sure thing."

It was between five thirty and six when the police report was finished. Detective Tate walked with Jawana and Holly to the front door. The sun was setting, and some drivers had already turned on their car lights. The temperature had fallen in the last hours, and the forecast called for a low of twenty-two degrees.

Tate shook Holly's hand and smiled at Jawana.

"Y'all go ahead to the apartment, and I'll meet you there in my car. It's parked over in our parking lot."

Before Detective Tate left, he walked to the radio room and told Janie Brannon, one of the dispatchers on duty, that he was going to a location to take a missing person report.

"We suspect foul play, and I'll give you the location when I get there," he said.

He then walked to Unit 30, climbed in, and lit another cigarette. He made sure he had his notebook with him before he started the car—a light-blue Ford LTD that was unmarked, without any wire or glass that separated the front and back seats. There were no special locks. It looked like any family sedan.

"All set," he said aloud, his fingers sliding across the seat, making sure his flashlight was right where it was supposed to be and patting his Smith & Wesson stainless steel .38 Special in his holster.

As he passed the public library on Eighth Street, he remembered he had forgotten to inquire about the red berries that grew on bushes along the fence rows between Greenwood and Fort Smith. It wasn't a big deal. He'd stop by tomorrow. For sure.

He drove east on Rogers Avenue, turned north on Greenwood, and then right on Grand Avenue. The streets were not busy. It was Monday night, and most people were tucked inside in their warm houses getting ready to sit down for supper, either at the kitchen table or in front of the television. As much as Ray Tate loved his job, it was on nights like this he wished he could be home with his family. The holiday rush was over, and there was no money left in anybody's pockets, just a bunch of credit card receipts or sales slips—reminders they had gone overboard again this year on presents.

He found the apartment complex with no trouble and parked close by the Gentry truck. He called into the station, talked to Janie, the dispatcher, and told her he was at 710 North Forty-Eighth.

"Will you check to make sure a Larry Price has not been brought in to the detention center and also check at the desk in the basement?"

"What time we talking about?"

"Start at eight this morning."

While he waited on the dispatcher, he glanced around the parking lot. It was fairly dark, with only the lights from individual apartments casting yellow shadows along the sidewalks. He looked up toward the second floor and saw lights shining in only a few of the apartments. He decided he'd take his flashlight with him.

The dispatcher returned on the radio a few minutes later. "Nope. Nothing."

"Okay. Thanks for checking. Ten-six then. I'm out of here."

He climbed out of his car, flipped his newly lit cigarette in an arch of red, and pulled his coat tighter around his sports jacket. The only sounds he heard were the vague conversations and music coming from televisions inside various apartments and the traffic from Grand Avenue.

With his flashlight turned on, he walked first to the metal box that held all the individual mailboxes for the tenants. He glanced at the names and noted the Price's box, thinking a message of some sort might have been left there. Seeing nothing, he turned, and with quick steps, he headed to the Price apartment.

If anyone saw the detective, he or she would have seen a seriously determined look on his face. Detective Tate was worried that Larry Price had been murdered because he'd put an ad in the newspaper to sell a car.

CHAPTER EIGHT

Tate tucked his flashlight under his arm and knocked on the apartment door. He knocked again. Still no answer. He knew Holly Gentry and Mrs. Price were there because he saw Gentry's truck. He knocked again, and after the third try, he turned the doorknob. The apartment was dark, and he reached around the door frame, his fingers searching for a light switch.

The ceiling light came on, and the first thing Detective Tate saw was a revolver pointed at him. Tate held his arms in the air. "What's going on here?"

Thomas Simmons had come back to the Price's apartment to wait for Jawana to come home. She'd seen him and could identify him, so Simmons knew he had to get rid of her.

Damn, he thought, *this whole thing has snowballed into something I never dreamed of.* He hadn't wanted to kill anyone. He just wanted to steal a car, sell it, and be able to pay his college tuition. He wanted to change his ways, make his family proud of him. But now he'd already killed Larry. He wasn't expecting anyone to arrive with Jawana. She brought Preacher Boy and now here was a cop. Who else was going to show up? *How many people am I going to have to kill to cover this all up?*

Simmons grabbed Detective Tate's gun and handcuffs. "Don't try anything you'll regret."

Holly Gentry sat on the couch with his arms tied behind his back. Jawana sat next to him, her head bent low, shoulders shaking.

Ray Tate was a good Christian man, and he trusted that the Lord would guide him in this dangerous situation he'd walked into. He had often told his fellow detectives that he felt like he could talk anyone out of shooting him, if given half a chance. Here was his chance.

"You don't want to do this, man," Tate said. "My partner will be here any minute. The station knows where I am. If I don't report back, they'll know something's wrong."

"Shut up."

Tate pleaded, "Let these people walk out of here. They've done nothing to you. This girl here is studying to be a nurse. This young man works hard and loves the Lord. He's probably got young kids. I've got young kids. Those kids need their daddies."

"I said to shut the fuck up. Turn around with your hands behind your back."

"No, I won't do that!" Tate yelled. "I'm not going to do that."

Simmons shoved the gun into Tate's neck. "Shut up and put your hands behind you."

Tate did as he man said. He saw no alternative but to comply. He knew Poncho was waiting for him. He'd show up soon. Tate just needed to keep them all here—alive in this apartment until Poncho arrived. The man wasn't going to kill anyone while they were here in the living room. If he was, he'd have already done it.

"You need to just leave us here and go. Go while you have the chance," Tate said while Simmons placed his own handcuffs around his wrists.

"Jesus is watching this," Holly Gentry said. "He loves you just as much as He loves the rest of us. He died on the cross for your sins and my sins. He doesn't want you to break his commandments. 'Thou shall not kill' the Bible tells us."

"You," Simmons said, "Preacher Boy, stand up. And shut up. You've been talking about Jesus since the minute I tied you up."

"What are you going to do?" Tate asked. "Why don't you just walk out of here right now. Before the cops get here. Leave us here."

The man grabbed Jawana and pulled her off the couch. He held the gun to her head.

"I'll kill her first, if you don't do what I say."

Jawana's face was splotchy red, and her body quivered with fright.

"Where's Larry?" she asked between sobs. "Where's my husband?"

"We're all going to walk out of here, single file," Simmons said. He slid a look to Tate and said very quietly. "We're going to get in that Ford you're driving. Cop goes first, Preacher Boy second. The girl and I right behind you. Don't try to run. If you do, I'll shoot her first and then I'll kill you bastards."

Simmons pulled Jawana with him as he opened the front door and looked out.

"Okay, cop, you lead the way. Lie down on the floorboard in the backseat. Preacher boy, you lie down on top of him. Do exactly what I say or I kill all of you."

When they made it to the Ford, Tate balked. He tried valiantly to get out of the cuffs, but they were tight and cut into his skin. He knew the man wouldn't shoot out in the open, and he wanted to save the lives of Gentry and the girl. Simmons pushed him, but Tate didn't budge. This time Simmons knocked him on the head with his gun. It hurt like hell, but he still wouldn't move.

Simmons grabbed Gentry and told him to get in first.

"No, I won't go. You'll have to kill me out here where everyone can hear and see you. I won't go."

"Goddam it, I'm not going to kill you. I'll let you go. I promise. Now get inside that car."

Gentry was praying, begging Jesus to stop this man. Pleading, "Our Father who art in Heaven . . ."

Tate said to Gentry, "Go ahead, buddy. I think he'll let us go. He just doesn't want to be caught here with us." All the time, Tate was plotting. *If Holly Gentry lies down first, I'll have a better chance of reaching his ropes to untie him.*

CHAPTER NINE

Poncho Davis, the detective who was Ray Tate's partner, returned from his six o'clock meeting and checked in with the dispatch officer. He went to his office, halfway expecting to see Tate sitting at his desk. They'd been working on a robbery case and were close to solving it, and they were going to meet again around seven.

Poncho waited a few more minutes, and then decided he'd just drive over to North Forty-Eighth Street to see if Tate was still there. He only drove by, but since he didn't see Tate's car, he didn't stop. He figured they must have passed each other going or coming.

As he drove back to the police station, Poncho began feeling a little uneasy. If his partner was going to be late, he'd have called him on their radio. Ray Tate was a good cop and not one to blow off a partner by not notifying him.

When Poncho returned to his office, he got a phone call.

"Detective Poncho Davis," he said upon picking up the receiver.

"This is Burl Price, Larry's dad."

"Yes, sir." Poncho's heart skipped a beat at hearing the voice of Jawana's father-in-law. He sounded as if he were about to cry. Poncho cleared his throat and said, "I helped fill out the missing person report on your son. How can I help you?"

"We were supposed to meet Jawana at her apartment, but she's not there. She called us this afternoon and begged us to come to Fort Smith."

"What time was this, Mr. Price? When you got to the apartment?"

"We got here about six thirty, but the place was empty and the lights were on. We went over to Tom Gilbert's apartment, and he called the police station for me, but the lady, whoever she was, told us that Detective Tate and Jawana and Holly had left there earlier."

"Where are you now?"

"We're at Tom Gilbert's apartment, and we waited, but then we went over to the State Police Headquarters to see if they could help us. But we're back here at Tom's now. We're scared to death! Jawana's parents are here with me and my wife."

"I'll be right there. It will take me about ten minutes."

Poncho grabbed his jacket and quickly exited the police station. He radioed the dispatcher that he was going to 710 North Forty-Eighth Street. The street lights cast a white ominous glow that reaffirmed what Poncho was already thinking. Something really bad had happened.

When he arrived at the apartment complex around seven thirty, he picked up his radio and called in his 10-6. He noticed a brown four-wheel-drive truck with big tires—which he later found out was Holly Gentry's—parked horizontally in front of two vertical empty spaces, which he considered odd.

The front door to Apartment Number One was slightly ajar, so he hesitatingly walked inside. The front door led directly into the living room. He saw the two coffee cups Jawana had mentioned earlier sitting on the coffee table in front of the couch. And next to the cups was a large flashlight standing face down. It looked like his partner's flashlight. Poncho Davis could feel his adrenaline pumping through his arms, his legs, his shoulders.

He investigated farther into the apartment, looking around, noticing that it was clean and tidy, with no dirty dishes on the kitchen counter or dirty clothes tossed around on chairs or in corners. As a policeman, Poncho saw the insides of lots of homes, and this was immaculate, which told him a lot about the couple who lived here. They were a hard-working man and wife, who obviously loved each other and took care of their home. They were just starting out to make a place for themselves in this world.

In the bedroom, where the bed was made and the room in perfect order, the phone was still plugged into the wall, but the wires to the phone itself had been jerked out.

Since Jawana had told the detectives earlier that she knew where the papers were to the Gentry car that was for sale, Poncho looked around to see if he saw any envelopes or manila folders lying around that looked like they might contain important papers. But he saw nothing.

With his heart racing, he walked across the apartment yard to a home on Alabama Street and asked to use their phone. He called the police station and asked for an alert to be put out for the missing Detective Ray Tate, Jawana Price, Holly Gentry, and, of course, Larry Price. He didn't want to use his radio and alert whoever had stolen Tate's unit and kidnapped the threesome.

He also asked that a team be sent out to the apartment to take fingerprints and perform other investigative procedures.

Then he walked back to the apartment complex, where he found the elder Mr. Price and gave him the bad news.

"It looks like Detective Tate's police car is missing. His flashlight is on the coffee table. The phone's torn up. I've just called the station, and we've put out an alert. My guess is they've all been kidnapped. But we'll find them. By God, we'll find them."

CHAPTER TEN

Jawana sat in the front seat while Simmons drove. He held her head in his lap, pushing it deep into his groin area. She could barely breathe between sobs she couldn't control, and she was afraid she'd vomit because he smelled bad.

"Shut up, shut up!" Simmons yelled while steering Tate's police unit with his other hand. He knew Gentry and Tate were whispering to each other, plotting a way to get control of the gun.

The pistol he borrowed from his sister's boyfriend, Squeeb, lay on the seat next to him. Tate's gun and holster were tucked under the driver's seat.

"I'll kill her if you boys make a move," he told them over and over. "I'll spatter blood and brains all over this car, and then you two will be next."

Tate, the heavier and taller of the two, lay on top of Gentry. He whispered, "I'll try to turn on my side. You try too."

"I can't. You're too heavy, and we're packed in like sardines back here."

"Then try again to see if you can use your legs to lift us up."

"I'm going to roll to the right, and you see if you can roll to the left. Maybe my hands will be close enough to yours. Then if I can just get the rope off your hands."

But Simmons had the front seat pushed back as far as it would go.

They tried to roll until they were exhausted. They were too tightly wedged behind the seat, and Tate's weight kept Gentry's body glued to the floor.

Finally, the detective whispered to Gentry, "Conserve your strength. Once we stop, I'll try to knock him down after I get out of the car. I'll wait until he gets you out. Let's both jump on him. And then once he's down, we'll split up and run for help."

"What about Jawana?"

"She'll be inside the car. While I'm getting out, you tell her what we're going to do and for her to lock all the doors, and if he leaves the key in the car, to hightail it out of wherever the hell we end up."

"Okay," Holly whispered. "Let's pray."

"Hell, man, that's what I've been doing."

The road was smooth below them, so Tate figured they were on the interstate. He heard big trucks pass them. If they could just be seen, maybe one of the truckers would help them. Tate estimated they'd been traveling about fifteen or twenty minutes.

The car slowed down, then stopped. Not completely, sort of a rolling stop, so he figured they had come to a stop sign. The next road was rougher, and for a few miles, the inside of the car was dark. No lights from anywhere shined in through the windows.

The car bumped along for a half mile or so, then hit a gravel road. Finally, the car stopped, and Simmons exited through the driver's side door. Jawana was crying still.

"Stay put," he told her, taking both guns with him.

It was cold. No lights could be seen in any direction. There was a sliver of a moon, and a few stars peeked out between the clouds.

It took a while for Simmons's eyes to get used to the dark. He opened the back door, grabbed Tate by his feet and pulled him out onto the ground.

"Stay down and don't roll over."

Tate's face lay down on bare earth. He smelled fertilizer. Maybe spinach. He knew they were in farmland. A field. Nobody would ever find them out there.

While holding his boot on Tate's back, the man grabbed Gentry's ankles, pulling off one of his shoes and sock as he dragged him out of the car.

"You stay down too. Don't move a muscle."

While both men were on their stomachs, Simmons reached for their collars and pulled them up over the back of their heads. He shot each one in the back of his head.

Bang.

Bang.

Just that quick.

Simmons opened the passenger side door. "Get out, Mrs. Price."

"No, please, no."

He grabbed her arm and jerked her out of the front seat.

"Come on. I'm not going to kill you. Not yet."

"Yes, you will. I know it. You'll kill me," she screamed and fell on the ground.

"Come on, bitch."

"Before you kill me, tell me where my husband is. Did you kill him?"

"Nah, he's waiting on you at my house. Be nice and I'll take you to him. But first, take off your pants."

CHAPTER ELEVEN

All hell broke loose when the law enforcement communities of Fort Smith, Van Buren, and all the neighboring police departments, including eastern Oklahoma, got the word that Detective Ray Tate, one of their own, had been kidnapped in his own detective unit, along with Jawana Price and Holly Gentry. Patrol cars were called off their usual routes and told to begin searching for a light-blue 1978 Ford LTD, as well as the 1979 silver and maroon Ford LTD that belonged to Holly Gentry.

Authorities from around the area met in Fort Smith Police Chief Henry Oliver's office, mapping out a plan for the search. Fort Smith Police Captain Ralph Hampton and Major Bill Young were there, as well as Sebastian County Sheriff Bill Cauthron. Each man was desperately trying their best to determine where to look for the kidnapped victims. They had men combing all the major highways leading into and out of Fort Smith, on either side of the Arkansas River.

Ironically, the Fort Smith Board of Directors was meeting on the following Tuesday night to consider a pay raise for the police department.

Along about ten p.m., Fort Smith Police Officer Danny Honeycutt was driving through Central Mall, a shopping center on the eastern side of Fort Smith. He had already had a busy night because he was sent to the Price apartment to bring back items to be fingerprinted: an ashtray, the phone, two coffee cups. After tagging the evidence and bringing it back to the station for safe keeping, he'd continued with his regular duty.

He was patrolling on the side of Central Mall that bordered Waldron Road when he spotted, parked in the vicinity of the mall theater, a Ford LTD that resembled the car belonging to Holly Gentry, the maroon over silver car that Larry Price had shown to an unnamed man earlier that Monday morning. The car was four hundred feet northeast of Osco Drug, somewhere halfway between the mall theater and the drug store.

Honeycutt parked next to the car, checked the license tag number, and radioed the station. Within minutes, several police officers, including Detective Poncho Davis, arrived at the scene. The car was locked, so they arranged for a locksmith to open the doors. They also checked to see if perhaps Larry Price was in the trunk. And if he was, was he dead or alive? Every cop there held his breath.

The trunk, save for a spare tire, was empty.

The car was taken to the police garage to be fingerprinted and processed for fibers, hairs, blood.

The officers were elated to have found the missing LTD, but were concerned that the car was a stone's throw away from Interstate 540, which connected to Interstate 40. Had the kidnapper ditched the LTD and sped away in another car, with or without Larry Price, on Interstate 40? If so, he could be in Tennessee or Texas by now.

Less than two hours later, a Van Buren police officer, Michael Simmons, spotted a light-blue LTD that matched the description of Detective Ray Tate's police unit. It was parked at the Union 76 truck stop on Highway 59 and Interstate 40 in northern Van Buren. Officer Simmons noticed right away that the car was very dusty, with dust on the hood and even more on the back bumper. He radioed his findings to the Fort Smith Police Department and asked them to bring a spare key so they could get inside the car. He also wondered when Tate's unit had last been washed. All the dust seemed very critical to the officer. Had it been washed recently? Or was it overdue for a trip to the car wash?

Detective Poncho Davis rushed to the truck stop, which was a big operation with a restaurant and lots of parking spaces for cars and huge eighteen-wheeler trucks. Tate's car was parked about fifty feet from the restaurant and ninety feet from the service garage.

Poncho recognized the dusty car immediately, and he was sure that Detective Tate's car had been clean when he left the station earlier that night. Inside, on the dashboard, he found Tate's notebook and a pair of glasses that Poncho recognized as belonging to Detective Tate. There was also a matchbook with the name Good Value printed on it.

"Let's pull this car into a bay and dust for fingerprints," Poncho barked. "Then, put it on a hydraulic lift to look underneath it."

Poncho realized if he hadn't gone to that meeting he had to attend, then he would have been the detective who went to the apartment instead of his friend, Ray Tate. It could easily be Ray looking for him, instead of the other way around.

Three policemen examined the underbelly of the car. By this time, photographers who had been listening to the police scanners arrived on the scene and shot pictures that would appear in newspapers in Arkansas and Oklahoma the next day. A tragedy like this affected all lawmen, all parents, all brothers, all sisters, all wives, all children.

They discovered dirt and sand under the belly of the car. Also, there were tufts of grass that looked like the kind that grew in fields along the river bottoms. Officers obtained the mileage figures of Tate's unit when he left the police station at six that evening and compared it to the mileage found on the automobile's mileage gauge at the Union 76 station. It turned out to be fifty-seven miles. They took a map and drew the circumference that would equal those fifty-seven miles and vowed that by daylight, January sixth, more than one hundred officers and volunteers would be searching river land either in Arkansas or Oklahoma.

Ray Tate would have left a trail or a clue if he'd had the chance. He was that kind of detective. And he would have fought against capture unless he thought not doing so would save others.

Officers were hoping they would find something Tate had dropped. They may have even been remembering the Grimm's fairy tale of Hansel and Gretel leaving pieces of bread as a trail to find their way home.

It took time, but eventually all the relatives of the four missing people had been notified. Unfortunately, Howard and Odessa Gentry heard about their son's kidnapping on a police radio.

Near Cedarville, Arkansas, in the early morning hours before the sun had risen over White Water Ranch, Holly Gentry's mama called her other son in Springfield, Missouri.

"Son, they think Holly's been kidnapped. Can you come home?"

Mark had been sound asleep when the call came, but the news jarred him awake.

"Kidnapped?"

"We think so. We don't know what to think."

"Well, what happened?"

"You know Jawana Price? Holly's part-time secretary? Well, her husband didn't show up for lunch yesterday, so Holly got the police to go looking for him. Neither Holly or Jawana or the police officer have been seen since."

His mother began to cry, hard gulping tears that rendered her unable to talk anymore.

"Okay, Mother, I'll be right down. I'll be there in a few hours."

On the almost three-hour drive to his parents' home, Mark thought about the terrifying experience he'd had the day before while taking a shower. As he was rinsing off, he saw flashes of red that appeared to be coming from the shower head. An oppressive gloom had swept over him, an evil presence that he felt was a vision of his own death.

He'd dressed quickly and gone outside to his backyard where he was alone and he could raise his voice to the devil.

"Nothing you can do, Satan, will deter me or my family from working for the Lord. So you leave me alone." And then he'd shouted, "I'm not afraid of you!"

He'd not shared any of this with his wife, Cynthia, or their children, Carrie and Zane. Usually, the family shared everything, but this apparition he'd kept to himself.

Now, on the way home with the news that his brother had been kidnapped, Mark realized that this dream or whatever was not a vision of his death, but it was a vision of Holly's death.

When he arrived at his parent's ranch, he was briefed on what all had transpired since Holly's disappearance. It was a whirlwind of explanations and suppositions tossed wildly around.

Later, after a fog had lifted shortly before noon, Mark rode with Jewel Morris, his dad's good friend and business partner, in his Cessna to search from the air for the missing victims. They flew over all points north, east, south, and west of Fort Smith. They circled

Ben Geren Park, Lock and Dam Thirteen on the Arkansas River, the Moffett river bottoms, and the Kibler bottoms. They didn't even know what they were looking for; they just knew they had to do something. They prayed unceasingly for Holly and his friends and the detective who tried to help.

CHAPTER TWELVE

Just before Danny Honeycutt discovered the Ford LTD parked not far from the mall theatre, another scene was playing out in Van Buren, Arkansas.

At the Speedy Mart convenience store, Thomas Simmons was making a phone call to his sister, Leona Powell, in Kibler, Arkansas. As he stood at the counter dialing the number, he looked out on the Union 76 truck stop, which was located close by. Only the Waffle House separated the two. The clerk chatted with Simmons, who had first inquired if Van Buren had any taxi services running that time of night, which was around nine thirty. She told him she wasn't sure, but probably not. He thanked her politely and asked to use the phone.

When Leona answered, her brother asked if she could come to the Speedy Mart and pick him up. She asked him why he needed a ride. He told her it was a long story.

Thomas Simmons—or Tommy, or Daddy Tom, as his relatives called him—had been released on parole from prison to live with his sister and her five daughters in a little green frame house surrounded by a chain-link fence in Kibler, a little farming community east of

Van Buren and west of Alma. He'd arrived at the end of October and had gotten a job at Arkhola Sand and Gravel. He'd bought a little orange Toyota at Owen's Used Cars in Lavaca, Arkansas, and was making payments on it. All in all, the situation was working out all right. Tommy helped with the children and some of the bills, and he got to be with the youngest girl, Vicki, who was his natural daughter but had been adopted by Leona. He often took Vicki and her little friend from next door, Tina Willis, to get ice cream cones and for drives around the fields of Kibler.

The other girls were distinguishing themselves: Linda, who was a U of A student at Fayetteville; Brenda, who worked at Penney's and attended Westark Community College; Jeannie, who attended Van Buren High School; and Jonie, who was in the ninth grade at Van Buren Junior High.

Leona and her daughter Jeannie picked up her brother at the Speedy Mart within twenty minutes of his call. Perhaps as a peace offering, he suggested he buy a bucket of Kentucky Fried Chicken for everyone to eat when they got home.

After they arrived home, Leona set the bucket of chicken on the kitchen table.

"Move your books out of the way," she told the girls, who always studied at the kitchen table.

Leona reached for the paper plates she kept on top of the ice box and set seven down, along with a roll of paper towels, next to the bucket of KFC. She didn't need to get any forks out because they could just eat the chicken with their fingers.

"Y'all can eat in front on the television if you like."

"Got anything to drink," her brother asked. "I bought some pop the other day."

"It's done gone," she said. "I'll get some more tomorrow maybe when I go to town."

"Okay, but you should have told me when I ordered the chicken."

"There's sweet tea in the ice box. Or just plain water."

After everyone had finished eating, Leona asked her brother why he hadn't picked up Jeannie at school at six like he was supposed to.

"I'm sorry," he said but gave no explanation.

"And where's your car at?"

"In Fort Smith, parked close to the mall theater. I left it there for Brenda to drive home from work. I got a ride with some friends of mine."

"Huh?" Leona said in a tone that might have indicated she didn't believe him. "Brenda didn't work tonight."

"Well, I thought she did," he said in a snippy kind of way.

Leona sighed. "Don't you think you need to go get your car?"

"Yeah, I'll need it to get to work tomorrow, but I've got a hell of a headache. Will you go get it for me?"

Leona was tired, but she didn't want to upset her brother, whom she constantly made excuses for. It was getting late, and her kids needed to get their homework done and get in bed.

"Okay, I'll get Jeannie to go with me."

Leona and Jeannie, who was an excellent student at Van Buren High School and was the editor of the school paper and yearbook, went over to Fort Smith in their old pickup and drove the little Toyota home. Tommy was asleep when they got back.

The next morning, Leona made breakfast for her brother and packed him two bologna sandwiches for lunch. He thanked her for the breakfast and left out the front door.

Thomas Simmons reported to work at six at the gravel yard at Jenny Lind. He didn't mention the wreck he'd supposedly had the previous day, and his boss didn't ask about it.

Along about nine a.m., he asked permission to go into town to check on something concerning the insurance on his car. He left soon after and headed to Van Buren, where he stopped at Citizens Bank in the Cloverleaf Shopping Center.

The bank had just opened its doors when Simmons came in, covered with sand and grit. He leaned in at the teller's window, getting sand all over the sparkling-clean marble counter.

"My name's Thomas Simmons. I deposited a check yesterday, but I found out it was no good. I'd like to get that check. I don't want to have to pay no fee on no returned check."

Elizabeth Arnold, the teller, asked for his address, bank account number, and phone number. She jotted it down, and then she asked for the name of the person who wrote the check, and he told her, "Larry Price. It was on a Clarksville bank."

The teller recognized the name from hearing it on the late news the night before and reading about the kidnappings in the morning paper.

"I hope that's not the same man who was kidnapped yesterday," she said.

"I hope not too."

"Just a minute, sir. I'll have to talk with our bookkeeper. Her office is in the back, and she'll tell me if we can get the check back or not."

When Ms. Arnold walked to the back room, she talked to Mrs. Wanda Hicks, who was married to a Van Buren policeman, Assistant Police Chief Wayne Hicks. Mrs. Hicks recognized the name also.

"Go back and tell him that the check has already been sent off, and we can't get it back," Mrs. Hicks said. "It goes first to Little Rock and then on to Clarksville, so it will be a few days. It will be Friday before he can pick up the check."

Ms. Arnold followed instructions and told the man waiting at her counter why they didn't still have the check.

The man left the bank, and while he backed out of the parking space, Wanda Hicks got his license number and phoned her husband as fast as she could.

"A man just left here. He was trying to get a check back that he'd deposited on Monday. The check was written on the Clarksville account of Larry Price."

Hicks asked his wife to repeat the license number. "Honey, you may have just solved a kidnapping, and probably a murder case."

Assistant Chief Hicks called the Fort Smith Police Department to tell them he was coming over with some information he thought would be important to the investigation of the kidnapping. All the way from Van Buren to Fort Smith, Hicks was smiling. This was going to be something they could tell their grandchildren about one day.

Sergeant Harlan "Skip" Sweeten had taken the call, and he and his partner, Sergeant Mike Brooks, met Hicks in the lobby of the Fort Smith Police Department. They listened to what Hicks told them about the man asking that a check written on the account of Larry Price be returned to him. Hicks gave them the man's name and his license plate number. The detectives ran the license plate and found out that it belonged to a Thomas Simmons, who lived in Kibler, Arkansas. They also discovered that Simmons had a record a mile long.

The three men went back to the Van Buren Police Station. With shaky fingers, Hicks dialed the telephone number.

"Hello?"

"Is Thomas Simmons there?"

"Who wants to know?"

"This is the sheriff's office in Van Buren. That's who wants to know."

"Well, he ain't here. He's at work."

"Where's that, ma'am?"

"Arkhola Sand and Gravel."

"Very well, ma'am. And just who are you? You his wife?"

"Not hardly. I'm his sister."

"And is your name Simmons also?"

"Powell is my last name. Leona Powell. And my brother ain't done nothing wrong. He's been keeping his nose clean ever since he come to live with me."

Hicks said his goodbye, but Leona slammed down the phone in his ear.

The police then drove to the sand and gravel business in Van Buren, but were told that Simmons worked at another plant of theirs in Jenny Lind, a little community southeast of Fort Smith.

When they reached the offices there, they asked Jim Pence, who seemed to be the man in charge, if Thomas Simmons worked there. He replied that he did and that he would go and get Simmons and bring him back to where the officers were waiting.

When Pence reached the site, he climbed out of his truck. He had to really yell because it was so noisy with boulders breaking and machines pulverizing rocks into sand.

"Tom!" he yelled. "The cops want to talk to you!"

Simmons took off his gloves and put them in his back pocket. Then he brushed his hands off on the knees of his pants.

"What about?"

"Don't know. Just told them I'd come get you."

Simmons shrugged his shoulders. "Beats the hell out of me."

When Pence returned with Simmons, the policemen began to talk to Simmons about the check. He was quiet and respectful to the officers.

They didn't mention the murders, but they hoped Simmons might fall apart. They also knew that Simmons had spent most of his life in and out of prison, and that the last crime he was sentenced to and paroled from was a kidnapping in Little Rock, in which he had left a man for dead in some woods after stabbing him multiple times. Miraculously, the man had survived and walked to a house, where an ambulance was called.

As their conversation continued, it became clear to the officers that Simmons was not going to talk about anything but the check written to him by Larry Price.

They asked if he would accompany them to Fort Smith Police Station, and he agreed.

While in route from Van Buren to Fort Smith, he was read his Miranda rights. When he reached police headquarters and was brought into an interrogation room, he signed an official paper at twelve p.m. on January 6th, 1981, acknowledging that he had been read his rights. He said his name was Thomas Winford Simmons and that he was thirty-seven years old and that his birthday was June 2nd, 1943. His address was Route Three, Box 219, Van Buren, Arkansas, but he actually resided in Kibler with his sister.

Simmons claimed he'd met Larry Price at Osco Drugs in Central Mall in Fort Smith on Sunday, the fourth of January.

"I sold him some pot and quaaludes. He gave me a check for three hundred and fifty dollars. I told him I'd get the drugs from my connection and meet him back at Osco at a later date."

"He gave you a check for something you would eventually deliver. That don't sound like any drug deal I ever heard about," one of the officers said.

"I seen him that night at the Union 76 station in Van Buren, and he told me he'd given me a check on a closed account."

The officers wrote down Simmons's statement. Of course, it made no sense. If someone told you a check was no good on the fourth, why would you deposit it on the fifth and then try to get it back on sixth?

He agreed to a search of his vehicle, a 1975 yellow Toyota Celica with a license number IFS 053. A Good Value book of matches was found in the seat of the car.

In the trunk, they found a blue plaid shirt from Penney's, size medium; a Craftsman hacksaw; an Old Hickory knife; rubber boots, size ten, muddy and dirty; plastic tie straps; cloth work gloves; a red plastic flashlight; and a cardboard box containing trash, such as food wrappers, paper sacks, cigarette butts, receipts, and an empty cigar package.

On his person was one hundred forty-four dollars and three cents. Quite a bit of money for a man who had hot checks out.

He also told them he had decided not to go to work on that Monday, the fifth, and that he'd driven around, had gone to Central Mall, and hung out at the Union 76 truck stop in Van Buren. He then asked what the problem was with Larry Price, and he was told it involved the kidnapping of four people. Simmons then asked for an attorney, and a public defender, John Settle, was appointed.

After Settle arrived at the jail and met Simmons, he advised Simmons not to talk to authorities about the kidnappings, which he obeyed. He was then placed under arrest on the charge of violating parole.

Later, around two thirty, two Fort Smith detectives questioned Simmons again. He told the detectives that he had been in trouble most of his life. He began to cry, and he asked that his sister, Leona, be brought to see him. The two detectives felt like Simmons was almost ready to confess, so they very kindly offered to call her.

They called his sister, but she said she was sick and couldn't come. In her stead, their brother, Frank, came. But Simmons didn't want to speak to his brother. Eventually, Leona did come, but by this time, Simmons was not talking to anyone so he was transferred to a cell in the county jail.

By the middle of Tuesday afternoon, the police in Fort Smith had already interviewed people who claimed to have seen Simmons in close proximity to 710 North Forty-Eighth Street.

Several residents of the apartment complex said they had seen a white male with thinning hair and bushy sideburns on several different occasions around the complex. Tom Gilbert said a man matching the description of Simmons came by the apartment on Saturday, the third, to look at the LTD that was for sale, but he told the man to come back on Monday. A taxicab driver said he delivered a fare from Osco Drug to 710 North Forty-Eighth around six o'clock on the evening of the fifth. Things were not looking good for Thomas Simmons.

And coincidentally, about the same time the police were questioning Simmons concerning the check, a bloody discovery was made in the Kibler bottoms.

CHAPTER THIRTEEN

By daylight on Tuesday, the sixth of January, members of the law enforcement communities had already gathered at various locations in a fifty-seven mile radius of Fort Smith. Along roads that led to the rich bottom lands along the Arkansas River, in both Arkansas and Oklahoma, policemen had stopped cars and asked drivers if they had seen any sign of three, possibly four people.

Volunteers from the 188th Air National Guard Unit, of which Ray Tate was a member, traipsed through muddy fields and frozen puddles of water, kicked apart dirt clods, and searched for any clues that would help. At designated centers, volunteers and policemen could check in and get a cup of hot coffee and a doughnut before heading back out.

Low-flying planes flew overhead, searching for what, they weren't sure.

Long about midday, Clyde McClure and his nephews were checking on some equipment on their farm land in Kibler. They were working on a plow, and Clyde returned to his pickup, which was parked at the end of the road that led to his farmland. On his way past a garbage heap of sorts where he'd dumped old equipment—such as used tractor tires, irrigation pipes, and empty oil drums—he saw blood. He figured some dogs must have caught a rabbit or something. He knew there was a pack of three or four that lived in an old shed he had on his land. He continued on to his truck, found the pin he needed to fix the plow, and returned the same way he'd walked before.

As he walked back by the trash heap that was next to a tall diesel fuel platform, he again saw the blood and, upon a closer look, something white in the midst of all the old junk. He realized what he saw was a wrist of a person's hand all bent over.

He hollered to his nephews, who came running over, afraid that something had happened to their uncle. Clyde pointed to the pit.

"It looks like I found them people the police been searching for."

They walked back to the truck and drove down to Westville Road. They flagged down a Sebastian County police car that was patrolling near their farmland.

"We think we found who you're looking for," Clyde McClure told the men in the police car. "Just up this road to where you'll see our fueling tower."

It was a scene the McClure men would never forget. It haunted their dreams for many years after.

Bill Bascue of the Sebastian County Sheriff's Department and Fort Smith Patrolman Randy Balch were the first to the scene. They later reported that they recognized Tate's clothing, so they were relatively sure the McClure men had led them to the murder scene.

Don Taylor, chief investigator with the Arkansas State Police, arrived around five that afternoon. He took dozens of photographs, from different angles.

The first responders thought there might be life among the bodies because they heard what sounded like a moan. They looked at each other. "Did you hear that?" one of the officers asked. But they then saw the source of the sound: a little puppy scampered away.

Fifty officers converged on the land. In the makeshift grave, it looked like four bodies had been stuffed inside a large tractor tire and then covered up with oil drums. It was a grisly sight that made even the most experienced of lawmen grimace and turn their heads. Others, newer to the job, choked back bile and gagged.

Trellon Ball, the sheriff of Crawford County, arrived also. A photograph of him—holding a flashlight, dressed in a heavy fleece-lined coat and Western hat, leaning over the bloody scene—was seen the next day in several newspapers. Since the bodies were found in Crawford County, this was now a Crawford County investigation. The kidnapping had happened in Sebastian County.

While Holly Gentry's brother, Mark, and his dad's dear friend, Jewel Morris, were flying over bottom land, looking for signs of the three people, they got a message from Grady Stone, a local flying instructor at the Fort Smith Airport, telling them to come on back.

Stone was waiting on the two men when they landed.

"They're all with Jesus," he softly said, like he was praying.

Mark yelled, "Praise Jesus!" He was afraid they might never be found.

Night had fallen by the time the crime scene was roped off with yellow tape. A cold wind whined across the Arkansas River, which was just south of the murder scene. Men huddled in groups of four or five, quietly talking, shaking their heads, and wondering most of all: who and why?

The Arkansas State Medical Examiners officers in Little Rock had already been called, and nothing could be done until they arrived. Nothing but wait. The minutes dragged by into three hours, the time it took for the medical examiners to travel to the scene.

The Kibler Fire Department drove a fire truck over to shine light on the murder scene, and later the Sebastian County Red Cross brought over a generator to supplement the power. A farmer delivered an empty barrel and a load of firewood in the back of his pickup so a fire could be built to warm those who waited.

The news media was there also. Newspaper and television reporters jockeyed for positions, while the lawmen tried their best to keep them at bay.

Some of the locals, who had farmed in this community for generations, arrived with the feeling that their farmland was somehow desecrated. They raised soybeans here, and spinach and seed corn. In the summer, tomatoes, cantaloupes, watermelon, okra, potatoes, corn on the cob were produced by this very land that had been turned into bloody river bottoms.

"What is happening in our peaceful little community?" folks asked. "We all look out for each other, go to church, support our schools, try to raise our kids right."

Evil had visited their world only four months earlier, when two men robbed the Staton Jewelry Store in Van Buren. They'd tied up a crippled man and his young daughter and shot each twice in the back of their heads so there would be no witnesses.

And now this.

It was a scene few of them would ever forget as they stood in their insulated overalls and camouflage hunting coats. The flames in the barrel cast eerie shadows on their faces while they hunkered over the fire, holding their hands palms down, stamping their feet to get the circulation moving, cursing the person or persons who would try to conceal bloody bodies inside a tractor tire.

It was close to midnight when the examiners arrived. They took photographs.

While onlookers tried not to watch, they were powerless to look away.

The examiners first removed the empty metal barrels that had been placed over the bodies to conceal them. One by one, they stacked the cans on the ground, out of the way.

They removed the body of Holly Gentry first. He had lost one loafer and sock, and a piece of heavy twine was wrapped around his other ankle. His remains were placed in a body bag and laid on a stretcher. The crowd let out a low gasp, and then he was loaded into a van.

Ray Tate was carried out next, handcuffed with his own handcuffs. Choked sobs emerged from the lawmen who were witnessing the corpse of a brother killed in the line of duty. He was placed in a body bag and carried into the van.

The men weren't prepared for the sight when they lifted Jawana Price from the bottom of the stack of bodies that were heaped one on top of each other.

"Oh, my Lord!" and "Sweet Jesus!" and "Lord, have mercy!" was heard by the waiting crowd.

Her clothed body was quickly placed in a body bag and loaded into the van.

Lying beneath Jawana was a .38 Special Colt Cobra 6-Shot with a two-inch barrel whose serial numbers had been filed away. Detective Tate's weapon was nowhere in sight.

It was close to midnight by the time their bodies were taken to Little Rock, where autopsies would reveal what had happened to the three people found hidden in the well of an old worn-out tractor tire.

But where was Larry Price?

The police were baffled by there being only three bodies found. Larry Price had last been seen by his wife at eight forty in the morning of the fifth. The best guess of all the investigating officers was that he was killed first, and then when the murderer realized that Mrs. Price could identify him, he had gone back to lie in wait for her to return to the apartment. Instead, he was greeted by Jawana Price and Holly Gentry, closely followed by Detective Ray Tate.

By this time, they all knew that a man had been arrested and was now in jail because he'd cashed a check, supposedly written by Larry Price. How could one man alone carry out such horrible crimes?

A cry of alarm rang out in the Kibler community. Women were frightened. Men, who normally hunted ducks and quail and deer, kept their shotguns loaded by their beds, just in case. Children were told not to leave their yards, and everybody had to be inside before dark.

The Fort Smith City Board of Directors met on Tuesday night, the sixth of January, for their regularly scheduled meeting. Mayor Jack Freeze suggested they cut the meeting short. He asked the crowd in attendance to join him and the board in a moment of silent prayer and then to recite the Lord's Prayer in unison.

A wreath had been hung on Detective Tate's office door, and a black ribbon was draped across the replica of a policeman's badge that hung on the wall above the door.

The room full of people knew that the police department was requesting a fourteen percent increase in salaries because of hazardous duties the police officers experienced in their line of duty protecting the people of Fort Smith. Who could dispute the need to reward the officers who daily put their lives on the line? The combined efforts of the Fort Smith and Van Buren law enforcement agencies had done a remarkable job of gathering evidence. They checked on every lead that came in, and their efforts paid off.

Ernest Kremers reported he'd seen Larry Price and a thin man with long sideburns and thinning hair looking at the Gentry LTD on Monday morning.

Michael Crabtree, who drove for Razorback Cab, was interviewed just one day after the disappearance of the four people. He reported that he had picked up a fare at Osco Drug in Central Mall (near where Gentry's car was found, as well as where Simmons's yellow Toyota was left and later picked up by his sister) at five fifteen and taken him to the Glenn-Holly Apartment Complex on Forty-Eighth Street. In the cab was an older couple he'd picked up in front of Sambo's, a restaurant also in Central Mall. The couple rode in the backseat, so Simmons, who was wearing a stocking cap, sat in the passenger seat next to the driver. Crabtree thought the man looked familiar, and that he'd picked him up and a woman with a baby the Friday night before. The passenger said yes, he'd ridden with him before, but he didn't elaborate. He asked to be taken to 710 North Forty-Eighth Street, so the cab driver dropped him off first before going on to Dodson Avenue, where he dropped off the couple at their apartment building. He had last seen the man knocking on the door of Apartment 1.

Donald Seaton, who worked at Phoenix Village Mall as a custodian and maintenance man, was out picking up trash around four thirty on January fifth. He noticed a yellow Celica parked a couple of cars away from where Jawana Price's car was parked. A man sitting in the driver's seat, who had long sideburns, appeared to be watching the car. Seaton was so concerned that when he finished his rounds and saw the car was still there, he took down the license number of the car. It was IFS 053. He told Mr. Jewel Morris about it, and he reported to Seaton that Holly and Jawana had gone to the police station to report Jawana's husband, Larry, as missing. They waited for Holly to check in, and when he hadn't called as he had promised, Jewel Morris went over to the apartments. It wasn't until ten thirty that night that Seaton heard about the kidnappings from the apartment.

Tom Gilbert, who lived in the apartments, was able to give a description of the man who had inquired about the Ford LTD on Saturday, the third of January. He drove a yellow car and had long sideburns.

Loretta Matthews reported seeing a man with long sideburns exiting a cab the morning of the fifth around ten thirty or eleven o'clock. Was this when Simmons returned for his yellow Toyota?

These people were asked to come in for a line-up that consisted of five men, all dressed in identical clothes provided to all inmates, which were dirty white short-sleeved tops and white pants. Four of the men were police officers whose description somewhat fit that of Simmons: approximately the same size, same weight, and all wore glasses.

The men in the line-up were each told to stand forward, turn to the right, and then to the left. They were told to turn around once and then step back in line.

Two men, Tom Gilbert and Ernest Kremers, identified Thomas Simmons as the man they had seen at the apartments on Forty-Eighth Street.

CHAPTER FOURTEEN

While the three bodies were being transported to Little Rock, Simmons sat in his jail cell in Fort Smith. He must have been thinking about his past.

One of eleven children, he had his first run-in with the law at age seventeen. He'd stolen a car in Hot Springs. Then he joined the Air Force, but he received a bad conduct discharge. He'd been arrested twice in Amarillo—and served six months for each crime of theft—and also arrested a couple of times in Oklahoma City for attempted robbery with a firearm and assault.

He'd married along the way, had some kids. In and out of prisons, he was unable to find jobs other than dishwashing or cooking at little two-bit cafes. He never stayed at one job more than three months.

In September of 1970, he and his wife and three children drove to Little Rock. They checked into a motel for one night, and he tried to rob a few places, with little luck. The next day, he took his family to the Salvation Army to stay while he slept in his car. On the sixth of September, he robbed a gas station on West Third and kidnapped a seventeen-year-old boy, Gary Wyllia, while he was working there. He put a knife to the boy's ribs and ordered him to sit on the floor board with his head between his knees.

He intended to let the boy off somewhere, but everywhere he looked, he saw policemen. Instead, he drove for miles into Saline County, where he spotted a wooded area. He then forced the boy out of the car and tied him up with a piece of cloth he'd torn from one of his kid's clothes. He stabbed him several times with a hunting knife, moving the knife back and forth until he felt the boy had bled enough to die. Then Simmons grabbed his hair, pulled back his head, and slit his throat. He left the boy for dead and covered him up with leaves.

His take was eighty dollars.

But the boy survived, got himself free, and walked for help. For that crime, Simmons got forty-five years, but he was paroled after eight, even after the prosecuting attorney—Jim Guy Tucker, who later became an Arkansas governor—wrote the parole board that Simmons was vicious and shouldn't be set free.

He was paroled anyhow, but instead of freedom, he was then transferred to a Federal prison for assaulting an FBI agent and stealing his car, a crime that happened about the same time as the kidnapping. The sentence was to run concurrently.

After another year or so, he was paroled for good behavior. Lorena had consented to let him live with her and her kids in Kibler. By the end of October, he'd gotten a job, bought a car, but his job at the plant closed for the Christmas holidays, and he was running short on money and had some hot checks out. He had taken classes while in Leavenworth Prison, and he'd already enrolled for the spring semester at Westark beginning in January of 1981. But he couldn't pay the tuition.

His life was never going to be any different. Here he was, in prison again, and he'd failed his family once again. He wept, thinking how he'd disappointed his little girl, Vicki, who had been adopted by his sister, Leona. Vicki liked to read, and she loved school. She had a real chance at a good life. Something he'd never have now.

CHAPTER FIFTEEN

In Little Rock, Egyptian born and educated Dr. F. A. Malak, Chief Medical Examiner, was in charge of performing the autopsies on Jawana Price, Ray Tate, and Holly Gentry. The procedures started at nine on the morning of the seventh of January.

Doug Stephens of the Criminal Investigation Division in Fort Smith, Sheriff Trellon Ball of Crawford County, and Don Taylor of the Arkansas State Police were in attendance, along with state officials and morgue technicians.

The procedures ended at five, and no breaks were held for lunch.

It was determined that all the victims died of a contact gunshot to the rear of the head, with the direction being back to front, right to left, and slightly upwards. In each case, their outer garments were pulled up and over the victims' heads, so the bullet passed through the material. The bullets retrieved from the heads of the victims were so mutilated that it was impossible to say precisely the type of gun they came from, only that they resembled those that came from the weapon found beneath the bodies, a .38 Caliber Special Colt Cobra.

A toxicology report determined that blood alcohol was negative. Drug screenings were also negative.

Neither man appeared to have been sodomized.

Jawana Price had not been so fortunate. She had been raped, both vaginally and anally, before she was shot. Her facial features were effaced because the soft part of the face had been eaten by an animal, likely a dog. The eroded area included the eyelids, the nose with its cartilaginous portion, the lips, and the buccinator muscles.

The hands of all the victims showed bruising on the palms and around the wrists.

Ray Tate had a large amount of bruising on his hands, indicative that he put up a valiant effort to escape his bondage. The knuckles of his left hand were colored with yellow and orange bruises, as well as the fingers and palms of his right hand. Deep blackish-purple bruises showed on his wrists, where his handcuffs had been placed.

Holly Gentry's right palm was covered in bluish-purple bruises, and his right thumb was heavily bruised. Grains of sand were seen embedded between his right thumb and right forefinger.

Sheriff Trellon Ball used a key to remove the handcuffs from the deceased Ray Tate, which must have been an extremely difficult thing for him to do. He and the other officers left after the bullets were removed and other evidentiary material was tagged, which included the victims' personal belongings.

Tate's badge and gun were not found.

Jawana Price's Timex wristwatch had stopped at 1:50.

Holly Gentry's Seiko watch was still ticking.

Dr. Malek estimated that the three bodies were killed after five in the afternoon on the fifth of January.

The families and friends of the victims were, of course, deeply distraught over what had happened to their loved ones.

At Westark Community College, students and faculty sobbed over the wasted life of nursing student Jawana Price. Calline Dipboye

Ellis was a clinical instructor in the nursing program. She praised Jawana for her intellect and compassion.

"She was such a wholesome girl. She had a big smile and a smattering of freckles that was very pleasing to everyone."

Fellow nursing student Janice Ray remembered Jawana as being curvaceously slender with dark shoulder-length hair and sparkling, round blue eyes. She dressed in simple clothes, like flare jeans and shirts and sweaters.

"I remember it so well," Janice said. "After class, a bunch of us would go to the library together. Then we'd walk over to Jawana's and Larry's apartment because it was real close to campus. She always made someone walk inside the apartment with her. And then she'd ask one of us to look under the bed and open the closet. Larry worked second shift, and she was afraid to go in by herself."

Howard Gentry said Holly was "the finest son a man could ever have." He had recently returned from a mission trip to Mexico with his church, Faith Assembly of God in Fort Smith. He sang in the choir, coached a softball team, and was leader of a group called Royal Rangers. For the past five summers he had taken the youth of his church camping in the Rockies. He was known by everybody as "an all-around nice guy."

Fellow detectives described Ray Tate as a "helluva guy."

"Nobody was more conscientious than he was."

"He went right by the book and followed orders."

"He was someone who didn't make mistakes."

"Never said an unkind word about anybody, and nobody ever said anything unkind about him."

Common refrains like that were heard about Tate.

One patrolman, Frank Hartman, said Tate would have done anything to avoid violence. "If anyone could have talked someone out of a potentially violent situation, it would have been Ray."

Ray Tate's children lost their daddy; his wife lost her husband. She would automatically receive a ten thousand dollar pension from the police force, and his son and daughter would have their college educations paid for by the state of Arkansas.

Holly Gentry's little boy and girl lost their daddy; his wife lost her husband. The youth of the Faith Assembly of God Church lost their best friend.

Jawana would never realize her lifelong dream of becoming a nurse. Future patients would miss her loving hands and gentle heart.

She and Larry Price would never make pretty babies.

CHAPTER SIXTEEN

Prosecuting Attorney Ron Fields was the elected prosecutor who served both Sebastian and Crawford counties. He was a decorated Vietnam vet, and he was in the middle of the investigation of the Staton Jewelry Store robbery and murders. That case had taken its toll on Fields because he had come to admire the Staton family, who had spent the last twenty-five years making a success of their jewelry store, the only one in Van Buren. Mr. Staton was crippled with arthritis, and he and his youngest of four daughters were closing their jewelry store when two men robbed and killed them.

That had happened in September of 1980, and now this multiple murder in January of 1981. Fields was weary of bad things happening to good people.

He would be charging Thomas Simmons with kidnapping and murder. He was fairly certain that Larry Price was dead, but until they found his body, he could only accuse Simmons of three murders.

And surely more than one person would have been necessary to overpower a detective with a gun, plus a strong young man like Holly Gentry, and then load them up in a car, along with Jawana Price.

Deputy Sheriff Bill Grill of Crawford County didn't get home until nine p.m. on Wednesday night, the seventh of January. He and Sheriff Trellon Ball had been interviewing witnesses and traipsing across muddy fields, desperately trying to locate the body of Larry Price. Grill had just sat down to a warmed-up supper when he received a phone call from the sheriff's office.

"We got a phone call from a guy who wants you to call him back at this number," he was told. "Guy says it's important."

"Let me get a pencil," Grill said. He was bone-tired, and all he wanted to do was eat his supper and get to bed. Grill took down the number and called the man back.

As soon as he heard the man's voice, he recognized the caller. His name was Lon Maxwell, and he had been a juvenile probation officer for a long time.

"I have information for you. I've been trying to get ahold of you or Sheriff Ball for a couple of hours. I want you to go look at something, and I want to go with you because I can't tell you just where to go."

Grill knew where Maxwell lived, so he drove there in his unmarked police car. When he arrived, Lon and his brother, Clyde, climbed in the car. Another man, a neighbor who just happened by, asked to go along for the ride.

"My brother come in drunk," Lon told Grill. "He'd been down at Clear Creek Park, drinking, and he seen something."

Clyde was still drunk. He kept saying, "A body or a mannequin, but I don't know."

Lon Maxwell directed Grill to turn into the recreation area at Clear Creek Park, which was about ten miles east of the murder scene. There were camp sites, picnic tables, and boat ramps for fishermen and duck hunters to launch their boats.

On that cold January night, the park was dark and deserted. Anybody driving into the area would be a little spooked.

Lon told Grill to turn right toward the picnic tables sitting along a wooded area that went down to a creek. At table six, Grill parked and left the lights on, shining toward the woods. He grabbed his flashlight and climbed out of the car.

He hadn't walked far when he discovered the body. Larry Price was on his back, almost vertically hanging down the bank, with his head nearly in the water. There was a circle of congealed blood in the mud surrounding his head, which indicated Price was bleeding when he was left for dead.

Calls were made, and Sheriff Trellon Ball arrived. After a cursory look at the body, he was pretty sure it was Price. He could see a trail of sorts, indicating the body was dragged down to the edge of the creek. He still had to wait for the state medical examiner from Little Rock to arrive.

"I don't want you to tell anyone who told you where the body was," Maxwell told Grill. "I don't want the press hanging around my house, wanting to talk to Clyde."

Bill Grill honored Lon's pleas because, as he later testified in Thomas Simmons's murder trial, "I was one hundred percent certain that Lon and Clyde Maxwell were not involved in Larry Price's death." In fact, Grill didn't reveal the anonymous tip until Lon Maxwell telephoned him a few days before the trial and told him it was okay to divulge the source.

After Larry Price's body was found late at night on Wednesday, the Little Rock Medical Examiners were called once again to come to the little community of Kibler that lay east of Van Buren in Crawford County.

As in the first discovery, law enforcement officers arrived at Clear Creek Park. They roped the area off. Pictures were taken. They looked for footprints, but since Price had been missing since Monday, and it had been cold and foggy with occasional showers, they were probably searching in vain.

Some people who lived near Clear Creek joined in the search. Mrs. Nellie Oliver stood at the front window of her home, waiting for her son and husband to return from helping the police.

"I was scared to death," she told friends. "And I won't forget that night as long as I live."

The examiners arrived and took pictures again. From the description of clothing given in the missing person report by Jawana, they knew what to look for. Larry was wearing tennis shoes, dark jeans, a plaid shirt, and a heavy windbreaker. As with the other three victims, it had been pulled over his head, and he was shot once in the back of his head at tight contact.

Farmers in the area brought in their tractors and made an earthen dam around the slough. Then the Kibler Volunteer Fire Department brought their hoses and drained the water. They were hoping to find more evidence or personal items of the victims. Nothing, however, was found.

Dr. Malak again performed the autopsy. Larry Price was seventy-two and a half inches tall and weighed one hundred and seventy-five pounds. He wore a silver wedding band and a Timex watch that stopped at 11:39. He also carried two ball point pens and one pencil, both made by Cross. Malak thought Price had been murdered somewhere else and his body moved to the position where his head was down and his feet upwards.

All the toxicology reports were negative for alcohol or drugs.

Yellow and orange abrasions were found on the inside of his left finger tips. Around his left wrist, where his watch was, blackish purple bruises covered his wrist where his watch band had burrowed into his wrist from tightly tied ropes.

His personal effects were released to the authorities to hold as evidence. Each item was bagged and labeled, following exact procedure.

When the newspapers and television stations reported the finding of Larry Price, they also reported that the body was found because of an anonymous tip. That added to the mystery, and everyone wondered how someone could have possibly known the whereabouts of the body unless he or she had some prior knowledge. Would this mystery be explained when the trial came about?

CHAPTER SEVENTEEN

As in all murder investigations, clues were coming in right and left. Witnesses came forward, and it seemed that everything was happening at once.

On the day that Larry Price's body was found, an eyewitness came forth with some shocking and damaging evidence. James Davis, age thirty-one, was checking on a friend's apartment at the Glenn-Holly Apartments. The friend, who attended Westark, was in Huntsville, Arkansas, for the holidays.

Davis told police that he had witnessed an event that took place on Monday evening, the fifth of January, at his friend's apartment complex.

He explained that he had waited a few days to come in because he was in some trouble with the police, and that John Settle was his attorney, and that John Settle was also the court-appointed attorney for Thomas Simmons.

Davis told police that before coming in to the station to make his statement, he had first checked with his attorney, and another attorney told him to contact the police, that it was the right thing to do.

Davis said he and his wife were checking on his friend's mail, turning the heat up and down in his apartment, depending on the weather, and just generally making sure the apartment hadn't been broken into or disturbed. Davis said his friend had a weight set, and his friend had given him permission to use it, which he often did.

He went to his friend's apartment on Monday night, about six o'clock. He heard loud music, so he walked outside on the second floor deck to see where the music was coming from. By the time he got outside, the loud music had stopped.

But he noticed a pickup truck parked in front of Apartment 1, and a second later, he saw a blue car driving up and parking behind the truck. He watched a man get out of the car and walk toward the mailboxes.

He paid no more attention and went back into the apartment he was watching.

Davis stayed inside the apartment for about fifteen minutes, working out on the weights, before he left to go home to his apartment complex, which was a short distance away.

The following is his sworn statement:

"It was at this time I saw two males cutting across the grassy area, heading for the blue car. The first man's hands looked like they were behind him, and he was being pushed toward the car. When they got to the car, the man behind opened the door and pushed the guy into the backseat. Then he ran back to the apartment and got a stocky man. This guy resists, turns and twisted from side to side. This man's hands are also behind him, and when he was pushing this man toward the car, I came down off the apartment and got behind a large tree. It didn't take long to get behind the tree. I saw the second man pushed into the car, and the car door was closed. When the man closed the door, he rushed back to the apartment, and then seconds later came back out holding a girl, who was crying, with his left hand under her chin. Her hands were not behind her. The man placed her in the front seat of the blue car and he closed the door. He then went back to the apartment and came back out holding to his body what looked to be a brown sack of some kind and got in the car. He was in and out of the apartment real fast. He backed the car up and drove off at a normal rate of speed toward Grand Avenue. I took off for my apartment. I just thought they were having a domestic problem.

"I saw the man who was putting these people in the car before. Some time close to the end of the semester at Westark in December. I saw this man drinking coffee at the Student Union Building. My attention was called to him because of his dress, looked like a workman and it looked out of place. I saw this same man again during the latter part of last week. At this time he was looking into one car and I was going to call the police if he looked into another car. He looked for just a few minutes and got back into his car and left. His car was a light or dented yellow car. It was a little car.

"At the time the people were being put into the car, I did not see a gun, but the people were facing me as they came out of the apartment."

Davis ended his report by saying he had received no promises, deals, or anything like that. He was telling the story because it made him feel better.

This was, of course, valuable information to the police. Except for one problem: Davis had quite a long record, dating back to 1968 in Jonesboro, Arkansas.

And he had a history of mental illness, which probably accounted for his trouble with the police.

He also had been in the military and stationed in Vietnam. He was involved in the massacre of a village and had received a court marshal.

Many interviews were carried out, some in the police stations and some in people's homes. A number of detectives and attorneys with the prosecutor's office were knocking on doors, asking questions.

Leona gave permission for the police to search her home. In Thomas Simmons's room, they found a blue shirt, a carton of Marlboro cigarettes with three packs left, a Good Value book of matches, cigarette butts in an ashtray by his bed, an empty cigar package, and one pair of dirty socks. When they looked in a shed outside the home, they found a box of .22 caliber shells, a roll of surgical tape, and a ski mask. These items were found between two stored mattresses.

Of course, the cops were looking for Tate's weapon, his badge, the men's billfolds, and Jawana's purse. They hoped to find bloody clothes—or bloody boots or bloody gloves.

Another interview took place in police headquarters. Of particular interest was the fifth-grade child of Simmons, who had been adopted by Leona. Word had gotten to the authorities that Vicki had told some of her friends at school that on the night of the murders there was a lot of excitement at her house. She was questioned, but she also had a legal representative listening in, acting as her advocate. His name was Sam Hugh Park, and he would be in trouble with the police, himself, in five months, accused of the murder of his mother.

They asked Vicki about her mother's boyfriend, John Neal Bryant, nicknamed Squeeb. It turned out that the pistol found with the bodies was the same pistol that Bryant had claimed in a police report had been stolen three years earlier. They asked Vicki if she had ever seen her "Daddy Tom" with a gun, and she emphatically said he didn't touch a gun because it was against his parole rules.

She also remembered that a long time ago, when they first moved to Kibler, that they had been bothered by a peeping Tom, and Bryant had given her mother a gun. But she gave the gun back to Bryant, and she guessed that was the one he later lost.

Bryant had an alibi. He was hunting in Mississippi with some friends. And he went to great lengths explaining how and when his gun was stolen—and he most definitely reported it to the police.

Michelle McClure, the teenage daughter of Jimmy McClure, was interviewed at her residence, which sat on a little rise above the crime scene about a half mile from where her uncle had found the three bodies. She was alone at her home watching television on the night of January fifth while her parents were shopping, and she remembered hearing what she thought were car doors slamming, but because their dogs didn't bark, she wasn't for sure what the sounds were. But they happened in two quick bangs, and then several minutes later, another bang. She got scared and called her boyfriend and retreated into her bedroom until her parents came home. She guessed the time was about seven or seven thirty.

Eldon Richards, who lived on Route 3 in Kibler, claimed that on Monday evening, the fifth of January, between seven and eight o'clock, he saw a car drive by his house going south at a slow rate of speed, occasionally stopping, as if looking for something or someone. Fifteen minutes later, he saw the car go by again, only this time going the opposite direction. He walked out on his porch and saw three people in the front seat and one in the back. He watched it drive by his mother's house. The car was a regular-sized sedan, and he thought its color was gray.

CHAPTER EIGHTEEN

The funeral for Ray Tate was held at Grand Avenue Baptist Church in Fort Smith on Friday, the ninth of January. His burial followed the service at Oak Hill Cemetery in Siloam Springs, Arkansas.

Two chartered busses and over one hundred vehicles followed the funeral procession up Highway 59 to the cemetery, which was seventy miles away.

Law enforcement officers from Arkansas, Oklahoma, and Texas were in the procession.

He was thirty-three years old.

The Gentry family was overwhelmed with the display of food, flowers, and phone calls. Nearly every man who came by the ranch to pay their respects insisted that Holly was his best friend. Dr. Torsten Seubold, who was a chiropractor, gave each member of the immediate family a much-needed, relaxing massage.

On Saturday, the tenth of January, Holly Gentry's funeral was held at Faith Assembly of God Church in Fort Smith. The sanctuary was filled with family and friends, and a closed-circuit television served the gymnasium that held one thousand people. Others waited outside to show their respect. He was buried at the Morrison Cemetery next to his grandfather on his mother's side, Reeves Smith.

Holly was only twenty-seven years old.

Several days later, his brother, Mark, flew home to Springfield in his Mooney. His wife and children had driven home in the family car.

Mark took off from the runway at White Water Ranch, flew south for a ways, and then turned north to make a flyby at the ranch's home. He saw smoke rising from several sources that appeared to be camp fires. All around the home, he saw what appeared to be a medieval military with tents and stacks of spears.

He flew on to where he crossed a meadow, where he usually wagged his wings to signal a goodbye. He looked down and saw brilliant warriors, shining like the sun, standing guard all around his parents' home.

Once again he looked down, and this time he saw brilliantly blazing angelic figures staving off a siege from the mediaeval warriors.

Mark was not dreaming; he was wide awake. After all, he was piloting an expensive, high-performance airplane. The vision soon faded, and he eagerly turned his craft toward Springfield, Missouri. He had experienced a bloody vision about the time of his brother's death. Now, he had seen a vision of angelic forms protecting his parents from barbaric demon forces.

The friends of Jawana who were in her nursing school class were devastated by the news of their classmate's kidnapping and murder. They could only imagine her terror, especially because they knew how afraid she was to go into her apartment alone. Her friends and instructors wanted to honor her in some way, so eventually a lab room was named after her.

They attended the combined funeral of Jawana and Larry Price at the Lamar Baptist Church on the tenth of January, a mere five days after the couple said their final goodbye to each other.

Jawana and Larry Price were laid, side by side, at Brock Cemetery in Piney, Johnson County, Arkansas. Their tombstone was a beautiful marble monument that depicted two hearts joined together. Under one heart, Larry's name, birthday, and date of death was listed. The other heart listed Jawana's name, birthday, and date of death. On the back of the tombstone was engraved the copy of the letter Jawana read to Larry on the day of their wedding.

"I waited so long for your love. It seemed like a thousand years but you finally came along. You wiped away all my tears. Now today is the beginning of a life that we can share. Just take my hand and walk with me. Together we'll climb to touch the sky. We can have a home where love will be our guide. Together we're not separate. We'll be as one until the end and God will be our leader as our new life begins."

They were both only twenty-one years old.

CHAPTER NINETEEN

The farming community of Kibler, between Van Buren and Alma, was noted for its rich farmland. Much of it was owned by farmers like the Kiblers—for whom the community was named—the McClures, the Arnolds, the Newtons, the Gooches, and the Parks. The Park brothers owned a huge operation growing beautiful plants like ferns, roses, zinnias, marigolds, lantana, columbine, daisies, petunias, and impatiens to ship to markets all over the South.

Jim Bryant and his wife, Judy, raised poinsettias and shipped them to markets at Christmastime. Their neighbors were always amazed to see the rows of large greenhouses filled with red, pink, and white poinsettias. The sheer beauty of the flowers that represented the season was very impressive. Growing poinsettias demanded the full attention of the gardeners: a certain amount of light, a certain amount of darkness, and a certain amount of watering and fertilizing.

Other families owned smaller farms, and they hauled their produce themselves to markets across several states. Their incomes were often augmented by working jobs in furniture factories in Fort Smith or for big companies like Dixie Cup, Rheem, or Whirlpool. Missouri Pacific and Frisco Railroads had once employed lots of people, but truck lines like ABF Freight and Jones Truck Lines were taking over the job of delivering goods across the country over highways instead of railroads.

Some lived in Kibler because it was peaceful and quiet.

But the new year of 1981 brought unwanted fame to Fort Smith, Van Buren, and Kibler. The newspapers screamed about the murders. Television stations carried news on their morning and evening shows, complete with interviews conducted with everyday folks who lived in both Crawford and Sebastian Counties, who now made sure their doors were locked at night and their shotguns loaded. The Little Rock, Memphis, Tulsa, and Oklahoma City newspapers reported on the crimes daily.

KISR, a popular radio station headed by Fred Baker, was vigilant in its broadcasts every morning. Between popular songs like "Jessie's Girl," "It's a Heartache," and "Stairway to Heaven," Fred Baker was especially unkind toward Arkhola Sand and Gravel. "Who would hire a person like that?" Fred Baker wanted to know.

Jim Pence and Bill Scarbrough felt the hot seat most acutely. Scarbrough had hired Simmons, and Pence had praised his work ethic. A decision was made to think three or four times before ever hiring someone who was recommended by a parole officer. The president of Arkhola called Scarbrough into his office and said, "No more ex-cons, Scarbrough!"

Scarbrough recalled that Thomas Simmons had requested a visit before Christmas. After they'd shaken hands in a friendly manner, Simmons had asked if he could be paid early. It was the Christmas holiday, and the plant was closed for around ten days. Scarbrough had told Simmons he was sorry but that early pay was not permitted at Arkhola.

Later, after he'd heard about the murders, he felt lucky that Simmons hadn't shot him. He did, however, recall that Simmons had a "strange look in his eyes."

When Scarbrough read about the Price couple graduating from Lamar High School in 1978, he thought back to his days of playing in a rock-and-roll band named The Phantoms. They played at a graduation dance for Lamar High School once at the Clarksville Fair Grounds, and they'd had a great time. He always thought fondly about the little town of Lamar. Until now, when it would always remind him of the man he hired to do a shitty job.

CHAPTER TWENTY

John Settle, the court-appointed attorney for Thomas Simmons, began the arduous job of defending a man who was accused of four counts of kidnapping in Sebastian County and four counts of murder in Crawford County.

The crimes were widely reported by newspapers, radio, and television. A policeman had been killed in the line of duty. A young man from a prominent Crawford County family and a young married couple had been killed for seemingly no reason other than the attempted theft of an automobile.

The first point of business was an order signed by Judge John Holland to commit Thomas Simmons to the Arkansas State Hospital in Little Rock—to be observed and evaluated to determine his sanity and to see whether or not he was mentally responsible for his acts at the present time and at the time of the commission of the alleged offenses as charged.

The order was issued on the seventeenth of January, and the defendant's stay was not to exceed thirty days.

On the tenth of March, Judge Holland received a letter from the hospital signed by A.F. Rosendale, M.D., the examining psychiatrist, that Simmons's diagnosis was without psychoses. He had an antisocial personality, but he was not suffering mental disease or defect to such a degree as to make him unable to appreciate the criminality of his conduct or to be unable to conform his conduct to the law at the time of the alleged offenses.

Simmons parole officer offered up information that Simmons was considered an excellent prisoner. The prisons reported that they had no record of him misbehaving in jail.

Settle sought a motion for change of venue. He asserted that the defendant was arrested on the sixth of January and charged with kidnapping in Sebastian County and capital murder in Crawford County. Since the defendant's arrest, the *Arkansas Gazette Democrat, Southwest Times Record, Crawford County Courier, Crawford County Press Argus,* and other newspapers widely circulated had reported the circumstances surrounding the defendant's arrest and all subsequent proceedings in the case.

Television stations—KFPW, KFSM, and KLMN of Fort Smith; KARK, KTHV, and KATV of Little Rock; and KTUL of Tulsa—had extensive audiences in Sebastian and Crawford Counties.

Furthermore, radio stations KAYR, KFDF, KFPW, KFSA, KISR, and KTCS had all reported on the circumstances surrounding the defendant's arrest and subsequent proceedings.

Settle said prejudicial publicity prevented Simmons from getting a fair trial due to the massive publicity the inhabitants of Crawford and Sebastian County had been inundated with, including details of Simmons's prior convictions, which would have been inadmissible in court.

Prosecutor Ron Fields responded rather succinctly that the defendant was charged with capital murder in Crawford County and that the charge of kidnapping in Sebastian County wasn't under discussion for any trial setting or for motion purposes. He added that the state prayed the court would schedule a hearing on the matter.

The request to move the trial was denied.

Settle also made a motion that the defendant's vehicle be returned to his family. He stated that the police had ample time to examine and photograph the vehicle, and that the vehicle was being held solely to harass and inconvenience the family of the defendant.

Was that true? Would the police keep the car just to harass the family?

Did the police think Leona Powell and her children weren't being truthful and keeping the car would be a bargaining point? Simmons's family was reported to be in shock that this tragedy had happened and that their uncle was accused of the murders. His sister, Leona, took to her bed, sick over it all. The girls were sometimes accosted at school. They were good students, and the teachers tried to intervene. Jeannie, in particular, was distraught over her uncle's arrest and the accompanying innuendo that was leveled at her and her sisters.

Vicki Powell, the youngest, was teased the most. She was taunted with "Your dad's a killer" and "Your daddy is a monster who killed four people."

One teacher recalled having met Simmons at an open house held for parents and relatives in the early part of the school year. They'd had a long discussion over literature.

"He seemed really smart, and we had a nice time talking about books and authors we both liked." Then she shook her head and laughed. "So much for my good judgment."

Neighbors of the Powells were quoted saying that the Dixie Mafia was involved and that Thomas Simmons was taking the blame in order to shield his family from retribution. The Dixie Mafia was a crime organization that had its headquarters in Biloxi, Mississippi. In 1980, they killed a judge and his wife there, and their sinister dealings were exposed. They dealt in gun smuggling, bootlegging, all manner of thievery, and murder. This organization was made up mainly of ex-cons, so it was possible that Thomas Simmons knew members of the Dixie Mafia. No link was ever proven, however, or their involvement in the kidnapping/murders.

A Methodist minister, Dick Halton, felt like the whole county was going crazy over the murders and blaming Simmons before they heard the true facts of the case. He didn't believe Simmons could possibly get a fair trial in Crawford or Sebastian Counties. Later at pretrial testimony, he took the stand to declare his belief that there wasn't a single person in Crawford County who hadn't already made up his or her mind about the guilt of Simmons.

It also became known that Thomas Simmons had made plans to attend Westark Community College. He'd gotten his acceptance letter but—and it was a big "but"—he had not paid his tuition.

Perhaps Simmons had wanted to turn his life around. Perhaps he spent more money on Christmas gifts for his family than he should have. Perhaps he was going to steal the Ford LTD and sell it. With the money, he could pay the tuition, buy books, and get a part-time job.

Or perhaps Simmons was involved with other disreputable characters who planned to steal the car and sell it. If Larry Price had to be killed, so be it.

The psychiatric exam had stated he had an antisocial personality. A person who spent years in prison, trying to stay out of the way of trouble with other prisoners, might well have formed an antisocial personality for protection.

When the authorities requested and received documents from various penal institutions that Simmons called home, they learned quite a bit about his life. Somehow the newspapers found out about his record and made it front page headlines.

When he was seventeen, he stole a car in Hot Springs.

He joined the Air Force, but was kicked out.

He had committed crimes in Amarillo and Oklahoma City.

He worked at odd jobs in two-bit cafes but always quit after two or three months.

He cut the throat of a seventeen-year-old boy and left him for dead. He was sent to prison for forty-five years but was paroled after eight.

He assaulted an FBI agent and stole his gun and served just under a year in Leavenworth.

His father was dead, and his mother, Eugene, had married Claude Bray. They lived in LeQuire, Oklahoma.

He had five brothers whose occupations were listed as laborers or truck drivers.

He had four living sisters whose occupations were listed as housewives. One sister was deceased.

Prison records revealed he smoked and drank, but that he denied using drugs.

Statistically, those who commit acts of violence have a common backstory. There are warning signs that often start in childhood. Most killers are male; in fact, ninety percent of them are. They tend to be intelligent, but perform poorly in school. Often there is no father figure, and a domineering mother raises the children in a dysfunctional home with many siblings. Frequently, as a child the killer wet the bed after the age of twelve, had a fondness for harming small animals, and liked to play with matches.

Thomas Winford Simmons possessed many of these traits, and he was accused of four murders. It was up to Ron Fields, the prosecuting attorney, to prove his guilt.

It was up to John Settle, Simmons's court-appointed attorney, to prevent that from happening.

Under the laws of the United States, Simmons was innocent until proven guilty.

Jawana and Larry on their wedding day.

Holly Gentry as camp counselor.

A PRINCE HAS FALLEN

Holly Gentry—

"He loved God,
he loved his family,
and he loved boys."

Article written about Holly Gentry.

Detective Ray Tate

FSPD #41 (Rev. 8/??)

MISSING PERSON REPORT

COMPLAINT NO. ________ CASE NO. ________ (leave blank)

NAME LARRY ALAN PRICE ADDRESS 710 NO. 48th #?

COLOR W SEX M DOB 4/1/59 HEIGHT 6'1 WEIGHT 180 HAIR BRN EYES Blue

COMPLEXION light GLASSES (yes) Gold Rim TEETH: GOOD ✓ FALSE NONE

PHYSICAL IDENTIFICATION ________ SCARS, TATOOS, BIRTHMARKS, MOLES, ETC.,

CLOTHING mole on Right side - scar on Right forehead.

LAST SEEN 1-5-81 8:40 AM DATE AND TIME WHERE 710 NO. 48th #?

REPORTED BY Tawana PRICE RELATION Wife

ADDRESS 710 NO. 48th TELEPHONE 785-4185

DATE AND TIME REPORT RECEIVED 5:00 PM → 3d Shift

ADDITIONAL INFORMATION Works Baldo electric. Last seen this morning as he left for WORK. Was shown another man his car the last time she saw him. WHERE PERSON WORKS, SCHOOL, POSSIBLE DESTINATION, ETC.

CLOSE FRIENDS: Jas Taylor ADDRESS 1913 N. 48th circle

ADDRESS ________

OFFICER RECEIVING REPORT ________

*FOLLOW-UP ONLY

*DATE RE-CHECKED ________ *OFFICER ________

*OFFICER ________

*OFFICER ________

*OFFICER ________

*OFFICER ________ light

*OFFICER ________ olive [illegible]

DATE CANCELLED ________ BY WHOM ________

1979 LTD maroon SILVER → Possibly in This car. W/M / 48 [illegible] 6' - DARK hair mustache 160lb

Copy of missing person report taken by Detectives Ray Tate and Poncho Davis.

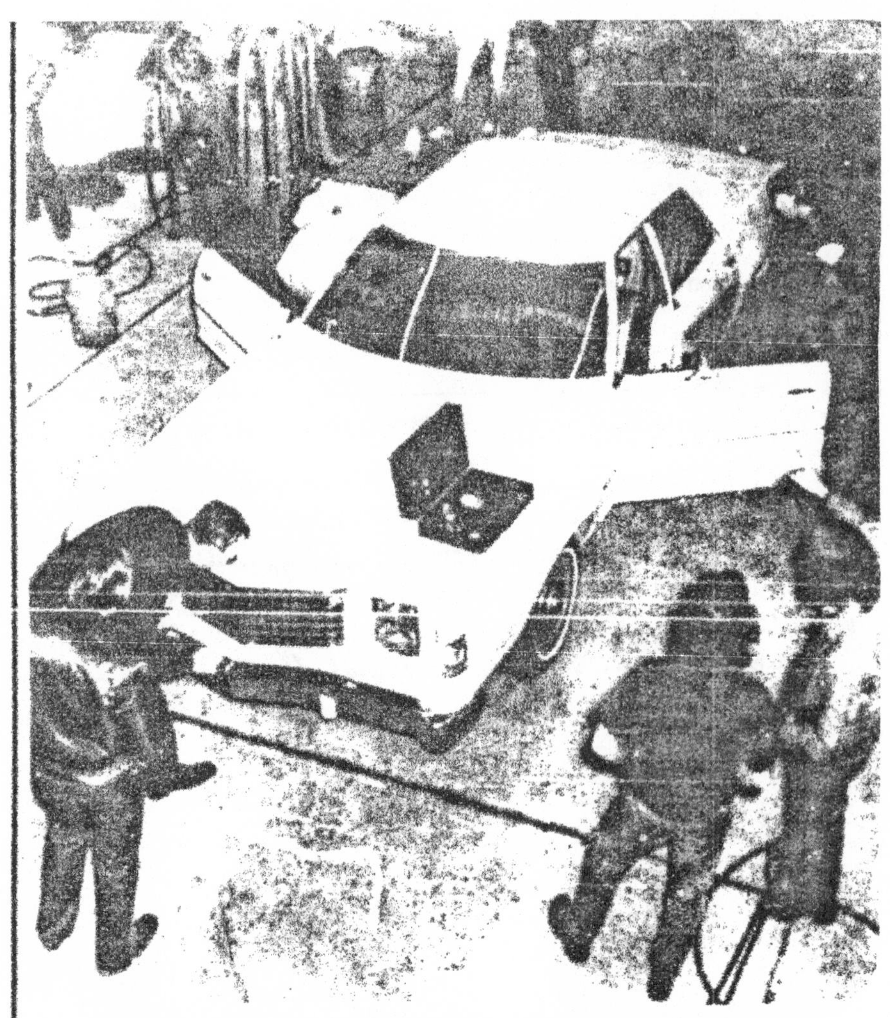

Police officers examine a Fort Smith detective unit found abandoned late Monday at the Union 76 truck stop at the north edge of Van Buren. The car's driver, 33-year-old detective Ray Tate, has been missing since shortly after 6 p.m. Monday when he went to a northside apartment complex to investigate a missing person report. Three other persons are missing in what police believe are related disappearances. (SWTR photos)

Law enforcement officers examine Detective Tate's car found abandoned at the Union 76 station

Simmons, clad in jail clothing, following arrest

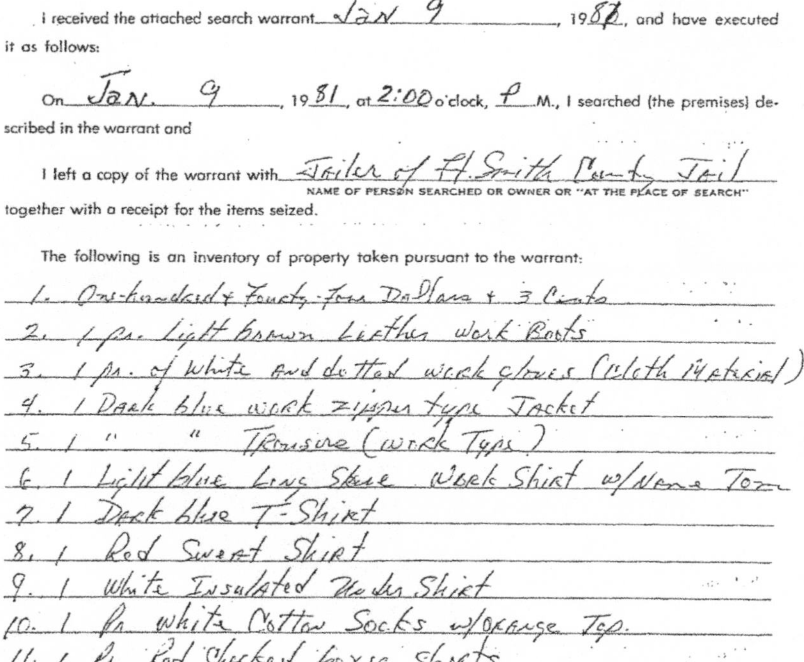

Return

I received the attached search warrant Jan 9, 1981, and have executed it as follows:

On Jan. 9, 1981, at 2:00 o'clock, P M., I searched (the premises) described in the warrant and

I left a copy of the warrant with Jailer of Ft. Smith County Jail
NAME OF PERSON SEARCHED OR OWNER OR "AT THE PLACE OF SEARCH"
together with a receipt for the items seized.

The following is an inventory of property taken pursuant to the warrant:

1. One-hundred + Fourty-Four Dollars + 3 Cents
2. 1 pr. light brown Leather Work Boots
3. 1 pr. of white and dotted work gloves (Cloth Material)
4. 1 Dark blue work zipper type Jacket
5. 1 " " Trousers (work Type)
6. 1 Light blue Long Sleeve Work Shirt w/Name Tom
7. 1 Dark blue T-Shirt
8. 1 Red Sweat Shirt
9. 1 White Insulated Under Shirt
10. 1 Pr white Cotton Socks w/Orange Top.
11. 1 Pr. Red Checked boxer shorts.

List of items found in Simmons's possession.

Jawana Price's body after removal from tractor tire.

Photo of tire where bodies were concealed.

Holly Gentry's hands. These drawings represent the hands of all four victims taken at autopsies. Note the markings of various discolorations that represent the struggles of each victim.

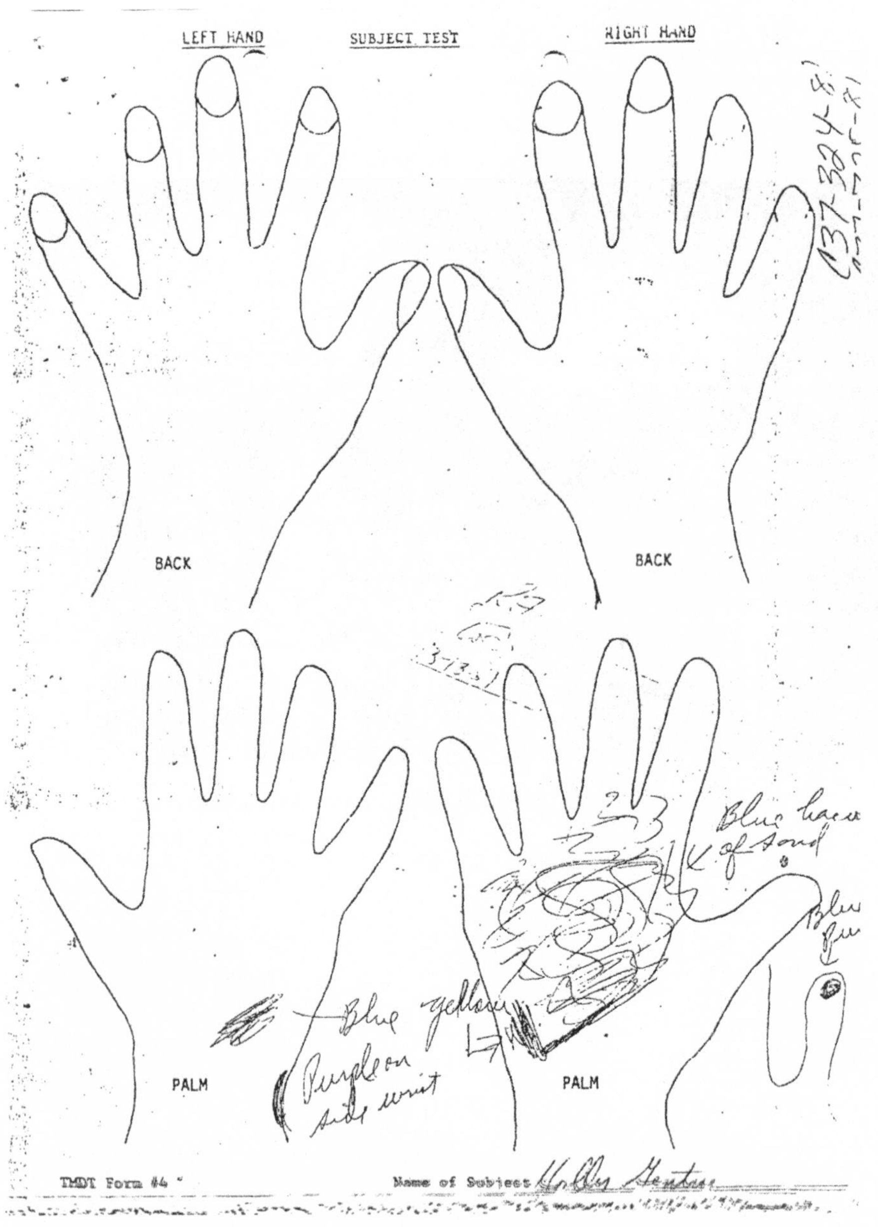
LEFT HAND SUBJECT TEST RIGHT HAND

BACK BACK

PALM PALM

TMDT Form #4 Name of Subject Holly Gentry

Ray Tate's hands.

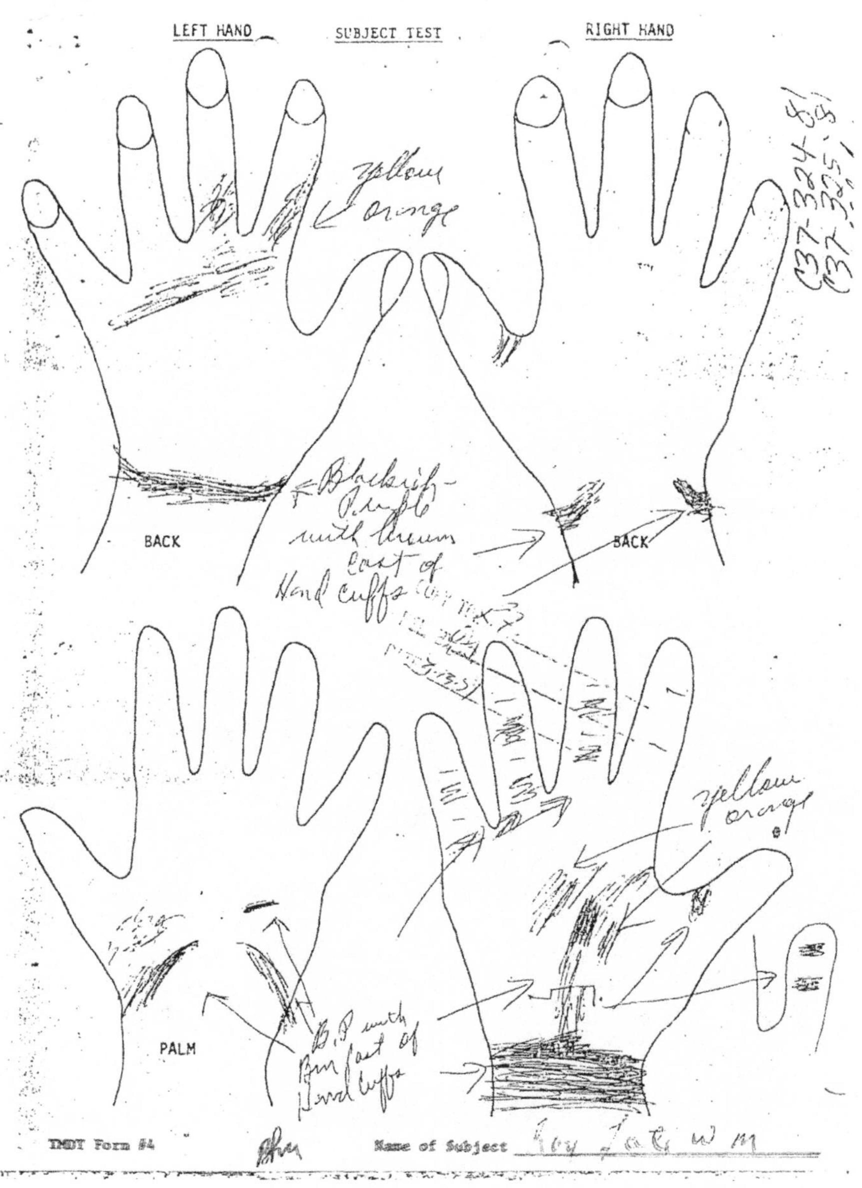

Clear Creek Park on a January day. Larry Price's body was found at edge of woods along the creek bank.

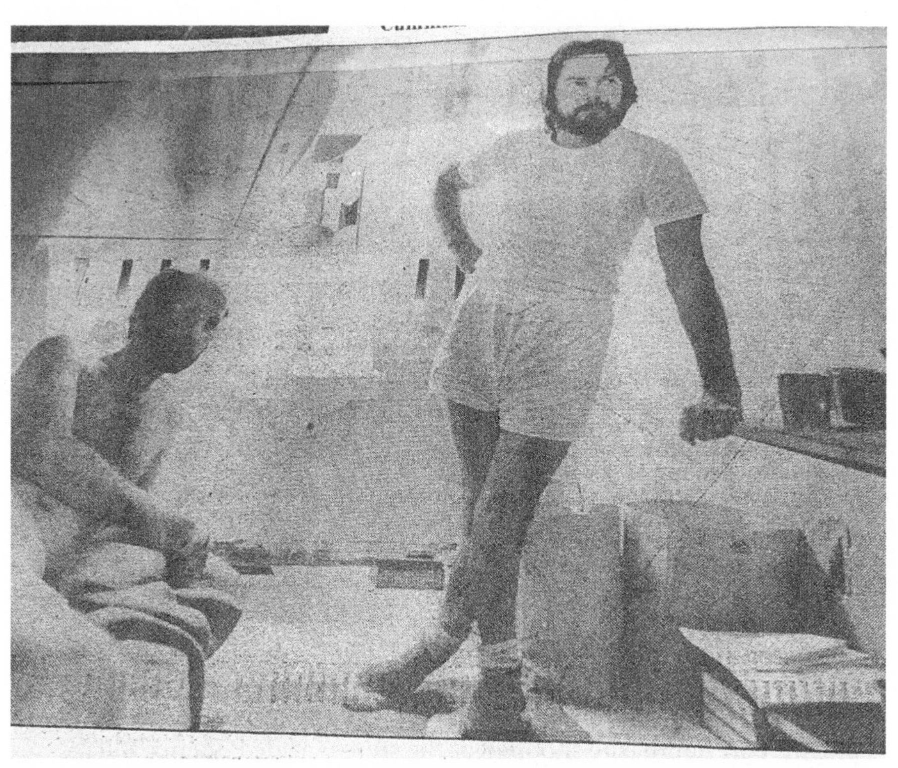

Simmons in death row cell (left) with Eugene Wallace Perry, who murdered two people in Crawford County in 1980.

CHAPTER TWENTY-ONE

Jewel Morris's widowed mother, Mrs. Nita Morris, still lived in Kibler. In fact, she lived very close to the home of Leona Powell. She was heartsick over the deaths of four people, who were killed in the little village she loved. She and her husband, Jewel Morris, Sr., had taught several generations of children who lived in this lush farmland community.

Mrs. Nita Morris was very proud of her son. He'd excelled in college and business. He was a good Christian with good Christian friends, like Howard and Odessa Gentry. And when she went shopping in Fort Smith, she shopped at the stores inside Phoenix Village Mall that her son had built. Not a mother anywhere was prouder.

Mrs. Nita Morris especially grieved over Holly Gentry. She and her husband had taught his daddy in school. She knew Howard Gentry would never get over the violent ending to his son's life. The irony that Howard's life began on this land, and his son's life had ended on this land, was not lost on Mrs. Nita Morris.

As teachers, Mr. and Mrs. Morris had a pretty good idea of how their students would turn out. Their behavior in the classroom—whether they studied or not, how they treated their classmates, if they lied or stole pencils or other's lunch money or got in fights for no good reason—was a good measuring stick for how their lives would turn out.

Mrs. Nita Morris had Neal Bryant in school, but everyone called him "Squeeb." Her prediction that he probably would *not* turn out to be a good citizen had proved true.

Neal was around fifty years old, five feet six inches tall, and weighed one hundred and twenty pounds. He liked to hunt and fish and travel around in his little makeshift trailer he pulled behind his old jalopy of a truck. He was considered the slacker of the family because his siblings were good, hard-working people. His sisters, twins Reva and Treva, were good high school basketball players.

His girlfriend was Leona Powell, a single mother of five girls. Her wedding picture to her children's father depicted a beautiful brunette wearing glasses. Heavy and now forty years old, with graying brown hair, she had few prospects for boyfriends interested in a woman with five daughters. Leona had a limp and used a cane. She didn't have a job, but collected a disability check. She was intelligent, and if she'd had half a chance in life, she might have made something of herself. Instead, she was determined to help her girls succeed. They were polite and courteous, and they all distinguished themselves in the schools they attended in the Van Buren school district.

Perhaps that was why Leona accepted Squeeb as a boyfriend, and she agreed that her brother, Tommy, could live with her after he got paroled. A mother determined to provide for her children will do just about anything.

Mrs. Nita Morris admired Leona until her no-account brother got out of prison and came to live with her. Squeeb and her brother did a lot of drinking over at Leona's. In fact, Squeeb Bryant lived in his parent's house, also close to Mrs. Nita Morris's house.

When she'd visited with her son following the tragic events, and they learned that Thomas Simmons had been arrested for the murders, they both agreed that one man could not possibly have killed four people. He had to have had some help; and she had a good idea who it was: Neal Bryant, better known as Squeeb Bryant.

And when gossip spread that the gun that killed the four people had once belonged to Squeeb, well, now, that was the nail that sealed the coffin. If Mrs. Nita Morris had her way, Sheriff Trellon Ball would arrest Squeeb and charge him with murder, right along with Thomas Simmons.

Only thing was, Squeeb had an alibi: hunting in Mississippi with some other guys. And the gun that was purchased at Buster Brown's in Fort Smith that was traced back to him? He had made a police report two years earlier that it was stolen.

Mrs. Nita Morris and her son, Jewel, were not the only ones who thought Thomas Simmons had some help in kidnapping and killing four people. Folks reading the newspapers were scratching their heads in disbelief. Reporters writing the articles weren't buying it either, and neither were the television anchors delivering the six o'clock news. Bur Edson, the anchor man with Channel Five, certainly didn't.

And the residents of Kibler didn't sleep soundly for a long, long time. They sure didn't like to apologize for what happened in their backyard. Their pastors in their Sunday morning services referred to the murders and begged all their flock to witness against the sins that were plaguing society.

After church, over Sunday dinner of fried chicken or a pork roast or maybe just a ham sandwich, the talk was of the murders. How could one man get from Spot A to Spot B to Spot C to Spot D to Spot E to Spot F? The newspapers said he took taxicabs from one place to the other. No way could one person do everything they said he did without help from someone.

Becoming a court-appointed attorney from the public defender's office in a murder case was not easy. The client didn't have any money, or he or she would have hired an attorney. With an indigent client, there was no money to hire investigators or experts to prove your client innocent. And if his family was poor also, then they can't help either. Or won't.

John Settle, the court-appointed attorney for Thomas Simmons, asked the court for more than the usual two hundred dollars allotted for fees and expenses, to no avail.

He asked for another lawyer to help him, saying his client would be denied his constitutional rights to a fair trial if help was not provided. He won that battle, and Garner Taylor joined Settle in trying to come up with a defense for Simmons.

Settle and Taylor filed a lot of motions only to have them overruled by Judge Holland. And they had to prepare for the pretrial hearings that would be occurring in the spring, with the actual trial probably starting in late summer.

In early May, John Settle received a list of witnesses Prosecutor Ray Fields could call at any hearing or trial. The list was quite extensive and included:

- Clyde McClure, who found the bodies
- Jimmy McClure, who found the bodies
- Michelle McClure, the daughter who heard doors slammed the night of the murders
- Susan Matthews, who worked at Citizens Banks and deposited the forged check
- Elizabeth Arnold, who first waited on Thomas Simmons at Citizen's Bank in Cloverleaf Plaza

- Wanda Hicks, wife of Assistant Chief of Police Wayne Hicks, who worked at Citizens Bank and got the license number of Thomas Simmons
- Eldon Richards, who lived in Kibler and saw a sedan driving on Kibler Road
- Jim Pence, who'd hired Tom Simmons
- Tom and Carol Gilbert, who lived at the apartment complex and identified Simmons
- Vicki Powell, the natural daughter of Thomas Simmons
- John Neal Bryant, alias "Squeeb," Leona's boyfriend
- Leona Powell, sister of Thomas Simmons
- Mike Crabtree, a taxi driver in Fort Smith
- James Davis, who claimed he saw Simmons kidnap three people
- Bill Grill, who discovered the body of Larry Price
- Poncho Davis, detective and partner of Ray Tate
- Doug Stephens, detective with the Arkansas State Police
- Bill Taylor, detective with the Arkansas State Police
- Trellon Ball, sheriff of Crawford County

These names represented some of those who would be called to testify for the defense. Other lists included Dr. Malak, the state coroner, handwriting experts, blood specialists, and hair sample specialists. Any or all of these people could convince the jury that Thomas Simmons was guilty of four counts of capital murder.

Settle had to interview each one. He also had to go through the prosecuting attorney's witness statements. Ron Fields had an open file policy, so Settle was able to start questioning the witnesses.

John Settle went to the apartment complex and took Polaroid pictures of the apartments and the parking lot. He talked to residents and tried to find out if they were really and truly able to identify Simmons as being there either in daylight or nighttime.

Being able to see who was in and out of a dark parking lot on a cold January night at six o'clock was deemed sketchy at best. But after the kidnapping, a bright street light was installed that illuminated the parking lot. Settle questioned whose idea that was.

And he researched articles written by esteemed scholars that opined the unreliability of microscopic diagnoses in forensic pathology. He asked that these articles be admitted in evidence and suggested that Judge Holland read the material to better understand that there existed certain problems in having human hair, blood, semen, and blood stains introduced in court as evidence.

The pretrial hearings were held on the twelfth and thirteenth of May, 1981.

Both sides would be able to find out just exactly what evidence would be introduced.

The prosecutors said one man, Thomas Simmons, killed all four people.

The defense said Thomas Simmons forged a check and nothing more.

CHAPTER TWENTY-TWO

The capital murder trial of Thomas Simmons began on the fifth of August at the Crawford County Court House in Van Buren. Judge Holland presided.

Ron Fields, David Saxon, and Lee Kuykendall represented the Twelfth Judicial District of the State of Arkansas.

John Settle and Garner Taylor represented the Public Defender's Office of Sebastian County.

Two hundred potential jurors had been called. They had filled out information cards on their age, where they lived, where they worked, if they were married or single, widowed or divorced, and how many children they had.

The attorneys pored over the information, trying to decide which would be a good juror who might be more inclined to agree with their side. Of course, they couldn't really tell until they were able to question the potential jurors who were called to fill the first pool of possible jurors. Six people were called at one time. One was put on the stand to be questioned, while the other five were escorted by the court's bailiff to wait in another room.

In legalese, that is called *voir dire.*

Ron Fields began the process by introducing himself to the first possible juror. He then explained how the jury process worked and asked the question, "Do you believe in the principle that a person is innocent until proven guilty? And that before a person can be proven guilty, the state has to prove that person's guilt beyond a reasonable doubt? And in the event the state does not prove someone's guilt beyond a reasonable doubt, would you vote to acquit that person?"

Right off the bat, the first potential juror answered "no." Of course, he wasn't chosen to be a juror. Both sides realized at that moment that choosing twelve people to decide the fate of Thomas Simmons was going to take a lot of time.

And so it did.

One lady, after being questioned over and over by the defense about her opinion of the death penalty said, "I feel like I'm the one on trial. We're just ordinary people who live out in the country and don't get out much."

Another was questioned about her belief in the Bible that said "an eye for an eye" and "live by the sword, die by the sword."

If a potential juror answered a question about where he went to church with "Assembly of God," then he was asked if he knew the Gentry family because they were big in the Assembly of God Church.

Voir dire took a long time. Judge Holland was understandably annoyed with the same questions, asked over and over again, particularly by the defense team of Settle and Taylor. They kept asking each juror if he or she read the papers, listened to television, and had already formed an opinion about the guilt of Thomas Simmons.

For the spectators in the court room, the process of choosing a jury seemed to hinge on whether twelve people could be found in Crawford County who had no opinion whatsoever about the man accused of killing four people or whether or not the death penalty should be the proper punishment for murder.

The defense team had asked the judge for a change of venue. It seemed they wanted to prove to the judge that he should have granted it.

The Crawford County Courthouse was a beautiful white two-story building on the corner of Main and Third Street in Van Buren. On the northwest side of the courthouse, an Italian marble sculpture depicted a bearded and caped Confederate soldier in uniform, shielding his eyes with his left hand and holding a rifle with his other.

August in Arkansas was beastly hot. People were usually praying for rain to come and water their gardens and cool down the temperature.

A fountain in front of the courthouse, surrounded by benches where folks could sit and visit, was especially appealing in the hot summer. Only the bottom—covered with slick green algae—kept mothers from allowing their children to jump in and cool off.

Inside the courtroom, the window air conditioners hummed loudly, trying to keep the big room cool. It made it difficult for some to hear the questions, and they often had to be repeated.

The lawyers wore suits and ties, and even the defendant was dressed for church. The judge wore a full black robe, which must have been hot as blazes.

White handkerchiefs were pulled from pockets and used to mop a lot of brows.

Everybody had breathed a sigh of relief when the jury was chosen. Twelve good people from Crawford County would listen to what the lawyers and their witnesses had to say and then determine who was telling the truth. Two alternates would listen to all the testimony in case somebody got sick or had a family emergency.

When court was in recess, the judge admonished the jury not to talk to anyone or to their fellow jurors about the case. Each was thankful for a break, but they really had no place to go that was cool, and so they often just sat in the jury room. Their conversations were about the heat, football, and church.

Ron Fields began his opening statement in his smooth, authoritative voice.

"The opening statement is kind of like the picture on a picture puzzle book. You can see the whole picture at first, and then when you take the pieces apart and put them together in whatever order you do, you have still got, you still have the picture in your mind, and you know, 'Well, this piece is going to fit here and later on it is going to connect up here.'

"Basically, what the state will do in this case is start with the day of the crime on January fifth, 1981, and we will walk you through, more or less, the hour-by-hour itinerary of the key people in the case, specifically the victims: Ray Tate, Jawana Price, Larry Price, and Holly Gentry.

"Later on, we will pick up the whereabouts of the defendant in this case, Thomas Simmons. We will start off with a police detective, who will tell you that in the late afternoon of the fifth of January, Jawana Price and Holly Gentry came to the police department in Fort Smith and that, pursuant to normal police procedures, when they were asked to report a missing person that they were referred to the detectives' office.

"The two detectives working at that time are Detective James "Poncho" Davis—there is another person in this case named James Davis also—and Detective Ray Tate. Now, these two men have been working as partners for a long time. They sit down with Jawana and Holly and take the details of the missing person report."

In present tense, as if his dialogue was showing on a movie screen, Fields continued to tell the jury that the Prices were selling a car for their friend Holly Gentry at the apartment complex where they lived and served as managers for the owner, who was also Holly Gentry. He told the story in present tense because he wanted the jury to feel like they were there with Jawana and Holly and Poncho and Ray Tate.

"And on that January Monday morning a man—whom she describes as medium age, tall and thin, with long sideburns—comes to look at the car. When she leaves for work at Phoenix Village Mall as a part-time secretary for Mr. Jewel Morris and Howard Gentry, she makes plans to meet Larry for lunch. When Larry doesn't show up for lunch, Jawana becomes frightened because Larry isn't the kind of husband who won't show up for a lunch date with his wife. Because she is in nursing school at Westark and is only working during Christmas break, they won't have many more times to have lunch together.

"Holly Gentry works for his dad at Phoenix Village Mall—sort of as a manager and has a business there—and Jawana tells Holly about Larry missing the lunch date. She also tells Holly about the man who came to look at the car, and that bit of information is very alarming because Jawana has called a friend at the apartment complex and found out that Larry's personal car is parked where it always is but the car for sale is gone. And Larry didn't answer the phone calls or come to the door when the neighbor knocked and knocked.

"So she calls Baldor, where her husband works second shift as a machinist, and finds out that someone called in for Larry and told the secretary that he won't be in. The secretary emphatically says the voice was not Larry's.

"By this time everyone is upset, and Holly leaves to go look at the apartment for himself. When he comes back, he takes Jawana with him in his truck to the police department. After they tell the detectives the whole story, Ray Tate and Poncho Davis are very concerned. By this time, Jawana is crying. Ray Tate tells Jawana and Holly to go on to the apartment, and he will follow them while his partner attends a meeting he can't get out of. The time by now is around six o'clock and getting dark. Poncho and Ray make plans to meet up again in their office around seven. Poncho goes to his meeting, comes back, and Ray isn't there. So he drives to the apartment, and when he gets there a little after seven o'clock, he doesn't see his partner's car, a Ford sedan just like any Ford sedan. He thinks he's just missed him probably, and he goes back to his office.

"But Tate's still not there, and he gets a call from Jawana's father-in-law, who's driven up with her parents from the Clarksville area. He says they were supposed to meet Jawana at the apartment, but the door is open, but nobody's there.

"Poncho rushes back to the apartment and finds that the wire has been jerked out of the phone, making it inoperable. His partner's car is missing also. Poncho Davis realizes very quickly that a total of four people have been kidnapped."

Ray Fields took a breath and let the previous information sink in to the jury. Part of a lawyer's job is to be an actor on a stage and to be a good storyteller, and Fields knew when to pause and let his words do their work.

The jury was listening, and nobody was yawning or looking out the window or doodling on a sheet of paper. They were with Ron Fields, hanging on his words, just as he wanted them to.

He continued his story. "That night of the fifth of January, the car belonging to Holly Gentry is found at Central Mall Shopping Center by the mall theater. Tate's car is found in Van Buren at the 76 truck stop, and it's covered with dirt, and grass and weeds are lodged under its belly. Fifty-seven miles are unaccounted for, and they begin an all-out search in a radius of fifty-seven miles where it's dirty and weedy. The search continues into the next day."

Fields told the story like John Grisham writes a book. The jurors were hooked, and they wanted to know what came next.

The prosecutor then took a step back and asked the jury to backtrack with him to ten o'clock the morning of the fifth of January, when everything really started.

"Thomas Simmons, instead of going to work, calls in and says he's had a wreck and can't make it in to work at Arkhola Sand and Gravel plant out at Lavaca. At ten o'clock, he deposits a check at a bank on Industrial Park Road, about three miles from where he lives in Kibler, for three hundred and fifty dollars written to him and signed by Larry Price on a bank in Clarksville.

"At four thirty that same afternoon, he's observed sitting in a yellow Toyota, watching the car belonging to Jawana that is parked in the back parking lot of Phoenix Village—not where Holly Gentry parks. He parks in the front lot.

"At five thirty p.m., a cab driver picks up Simmons at Central Mall and takes him to the apartment complex where the Prices live.

"At nine thirty p.m., Simmons calls his sister in Kibler and asks her to come pick him up at the Speedy Mart in Van Buren, near the 76 truck stop in Van Buren. He tells her he got a ride with friends because he left his car at Central Mall near the mall theater, and because he has a splitting headache, will she go pick it up so he'll have a way to get to work the next morning? He doesn't tell his sister that he didn't work that Monday or that he'd been in a wreck. He tells her he left his car for his niece, who works the evening shift at Penney's, but she wasn't even working that night.

"The next morning, Simmons does go to work, but he asks for a little time off at nine o'clock, the opening times for banks in Van Buren, and he goes to Citizens Bank at Cloverleaf Plaza and asks for the check he deposited the day before. He wants it returned because he's found out it's no good. Well, it so happens that the lady in the bank is familiar with the name 'Larry Price' because her boss's husband is a Van Buren cop, and she's heard all about the man's kidnapping. She tells the man he can't have the check back until Friday because it's already been sent out. Her boss looks out the window when Simmons leaves and gets his license number and calls her husband.

"The police find out where he works and goes to Lavaca and picks him up and takes him to Fort Smith because Larry Price was kidnapped from Fort Smith."

Ron Fields paused again and let the information about Thomas Simmons soak in. After he walked to the podium, he checked his notes and returned to look at the jury.

"On the same afternoon, Simmons is in custody in Fort Smith, a farmer in the Kibler bottoms finds three dead bodies in a pile, partially hidden in a tractor tire on his land. It turns out to be Jawana, Holly, and Ray Tate. A pistol is found with the bodies that ballistics say is consistent with bullets fired from that weapon.

"The next night, Larry Price's body is found in Clear Creek Park, which is only a few miles from where the first three bodies were found. He was killed with the same gun."

He ended his opening with salacious findings that were hard for Jawana's parents and in-laws to hear.

"When the examiner conducts his autopsy on Jawana Price, it appears that she has been raped, both normal intercourse and also anally. There will also be some testimony about how they determined that. The sperm is found. Pantyhose are inside out. The belt loops are missing when the belt is put back through. So it appears that all three people were not killed simultaneously."

Fields thanked the jury for their attention and sat down. He had practiced his opening many times, and though he was pleased with himself, he didn't dare change the expression on his face.

Judge Holland asked the jury to give their attention to Mr. Settle for the defense opening statement.

"Good morning, ladies and gentlemen. On January sixth, 1981, Tom Simmons got up at four thirty in the morning.

"Your Honor, is the microphone on? Can you hear me?"

The jurors nod that they can.

"Okay. He was living with his sister, Leona, and his nieces—Linda, Jeannie, Brenda, Jamie—and his daughter, Vicki. They lived in a little frame house near Kibler. He had to get up that early so that he could get to work on time. He worked at the Arkhola Sand and Gravel Company plant down in Jenny Lind. His job was to clean out the debris—the rocks, stones, and dirt—out from under the conveyor belts that came from these large rock-crushing machines. This is hard physical work. Tom Simmons was glad to have the work so he could earn his way through school. He had already been accepted, and he was planning on taking courses and continuing his education.

"He arrived at work at six thirty. At around eight thirty, Tom Simmons asked for permission to leave work because he needed to go to the bank.

"You see, ladies and gentlemen, during the Christmas holidays, Tom did something that many of us do. He spent too much money on his family, went a little overboard and bought more gifts than he really could afford, and was overdrawn on his checking account.

"He expected to receive some money owed to him by a friend, and as soon as he received that money, he was going to deposit it in his account.

"Tom went to the bank to pick up a check, to redeem a check, and that check was on the account of Larry Price. In fact, Tom had met Larry Price the day before. Tom had gone by the Price apartment the day before that morning, to look at a car for this same friend. He had gone by, and he and Larry Price took the car out for a test drive.

"When they got back to the apartment, Larry invited him in for a cup of coffee. Tom needed to make a phone call, and Larry told him to go ahead. The phone was located in the back bedroom. At this point, Jawana Price, Larry's wife, was leaving to go to work. Larry escorted her out to the car. As Tom was making his call, he discovered a checkbook, and he took a check. He talked to Larry Price for a few more minutes, and then he left.

"He went to the Citizens Bank in the Industrial Park area, and he made out the check for three hundred and fifty dollars, and he deposited three hundred in his account.

"So on this Tuesday, this Tuesday morning Tom went to redeem the check. He had been eating his breakfast that morning that his sister had prepared for him. He read about the people who were missing. He did not realize one of the people who was missing was the person he might have met the day before. He went, drove to work, and after he had been working a couple of hours he remembered the check, and he realized that this might be the same person he had met. He went to the bank, and he tried to redeem this check. When he was unable to do so, he drove back to work and went back to work on his job working under the conveyor belt.

"About two hours later, Tom saw two police cars drive up to the office at the plant. He continued working until he was interrupted by his foreman, who drove up in his pickup to the work site, and the foreman told Tom that the police wanted to talk to him about a check. Tom got in the pickup with his foreman and drove to the office. When he got to the office, the police told him they wanted to talk with him about a check. Tom got into the police car with the officers and they drove, he rode with them to the police station.

"Ladies and gentlemen, we do not know what actually happened to those people on January fifth, and we don't pretend to solve this crime, but we do know that Tom Simmons is not guilty of kidnapping and murdering these people, and we believe that when all the evidence is in, all of it, that you will agree with us.

"Thank you."

Ron Fields was surprised at Settle's opening statement. In fact, he asked for a fifteen-minute recess. Settle had begun his opening with the day *after* the crimes happened. He told the jury that his client forged a check, deposited it, and then tried to get it back. And he always referred to his client as "Tom." Perhaps he thought it a friendlier-sounding name.

Fields must have thought: *What? That's it?*

CHAPTER TWENTY-THREE

Ron Fields called Poncho Davis to the stand next, and he asked him to go through the evening of January 5, 1981, when he and his partner, Ray Tate, first met Jawana Price and Holly Gentry.

After his testimony, John Settle cross-examined Poncho Davis, mainly about how dark it was that evening when Tate left to go to the apartment. Davis said it was dusk and that some people, but not all, had turned on their lights. Settle wanted Davis to say it was dark because he knew there was another witness, a man named James Davis, who was going to testify that he saw three people led out of the Price apartment by a man and that they got into a sedan and drove off.

Fields then called Ernie Kremers and Tom Gilbert, who testified they'd seen Simmons looking at a 1979 Ford LTD, maroon over silver, at the apartment complex on North Forty-Eighth street.

Settle's cross was perfunctory.

Fields then called Carol Gilbert, who testified that she had received a phone call from Jawana Price, asking her to see if her husband was at their apartment by knocking on their door and also if the Ford LTD was gone. Gilbert testified that Larry Price did not come to the door after she knocked many times. Price's car was parked where it usually was, but the car that was for sale was gone.

Again, there wasn't much Settle could find out from Carol Gilbert.

Fields called Michael Crabtree, who was the cab driver who picked up Simmons at Central Mall at five thirty the Monday afternoon of the fifth of January and took him to the apartment complex at North Forty-Eighth Street.

Settle crossed him fairly forcefully, wondering how he could be so sure that his passenger was Simmons since he had not been able to identify him in the police lineup.

And then, Ron Fields called James Davis, who had testified during the pretrial. Fields knew, of course, how Davis would answer his questions, so he asked Davis to explain what he saw on the early evening of the fifth of January. Davis explained that he was looking after an apartment for a college friend of his, who was visiting his parents in Huntsville, Arkansas, over Christmas break. His friend's apartment was in the same complex where Larry and Jawana Price lived. He claimed that he'd seen a man usher out, one at a time, two men with their hands behind their backs and a woman to a sedan in the parking lot around six thirty or so. He had even hidden behind to tree to get a better look.

John Settle couldn't wait to cross examine James Davis. Settle, in fact, had once represented Davis in a criminal matter. He also knew Davis had a police record and was mentally ill—diagnosed as schizophrenic.

He questioned Davis about the time he first went to the apartment.

> Q. What time did you go to the apartment?
> A. About five thirty.
> Q. You heard loud music?
> A. Coming from a station wagon.
> Q. Where was this station wagon located?

A. Between the first and second apartment.
Q. Could you see anybody in the car?
A. No, I didn't.
Q. Just loud music playing and the car was empty?
A. Very loud music.
Q. Did you see anybody around this car?
A. No, I didn't.
Q. Did you think someone put it there just to annoy the neighborhood?
A. Yes.
Q. This station wagon was between the first and second apartment, correct?
A. That is correct.
Q. I believe you stated that you went to the apartment about five thirty?
A. Yes.
Q. How often had you been going over there?
A. He had been gone for about a week. Between fall and spring break at Westark.
Q. Had you been going every day?
A. Every other day.
Q. Every other day?
A. More or less.
Q. Now this car that pulled up. You said it was what color, what type of color?
A. A bluish green, aqua colored.
Q. Green?
A. Bluish green, aqua.
Q. Let me show you state's exhibit number two. This photograph? Does it look familiar to you?
A. It reasonably looks like the car that was pulled up behind the pickup truck.

Q. It's a light-blue car, isn't it?
A. Yes.
Q. It doesn't really look green, does it?
A. It looks green to me.
Q. You insist on that, huh?
A. (No response)
Q. Okay. Now, when this car pulled up, where did it go in the driveway?
A. It parked behind a pickup truck.
Q. And where was this pickup truck?
A. Parked parallel to the driveway.
Q. Parallel to the driveway?
A. Yes.
Q. Was it in the middle of the driveway?
A. No. To the right of the driveway.
Q. The extreme right?
A. The extreme right?

The questioning went on like this for what seemed like an eternity to the jury. One could tell by the yawns and the moving around in the chairs and the fighting off sleep that they wished Mr. Settle would move things along.

Finally, the questions and answers arrived at the conclusion that a man drove the car. He got out. He looked into the pickup truck. He walked to the mailboxes that were close by.

Q. How long did he stand at the mailboxes?
A. I'm not real sure.
Q. You're not real sure?
A. I went back into the apartment.
Q. Okay. When he was in front of the mailboxes, you just left it there and went on upstairs.
A. I was already upstairs. I was on the balcony when he pulled up in the car.

The attorney and the witness continued to spar for another five minutes about whether or not the drapes were pulled on the window of the apartment the witness was watching. And if the lights were turned on. Or not. Finally:

> Q. Now this man, this man that got out. What did he look like?
> A. Blank.
> Q. Blank?
> A. Yeah, I don't have any recollections of what people look like.
> Q. You have no recollections of what people look like?
> A. No.
> Q. I see. So you can't tell the jury here what this first man looked like at all?
> A. I don't even know how tall you are.
> Q. Could you tell anything about his features?
> A. No, I couldn't.
> Q. Could you tell anything about his hair color?
> A. No, I couldn't.
> Q. Could you tell if he had facial hair or sideburns?
> A. Didn't apply. Didn't look.
> Q. Didn't look?
> A. No.
> Q. What was he wearing?
> A. A suit. A dark brownish-blue suit.
> Q. A brownish blue?
> A. A brownish green. A brownish suit.
> Q. A dark suit? What else was he wearing?
> A. A coat.
> Q. Do you recall the color of the coat?

A. No. I don't.

This bizarre testimony continued. To the jurors, the judge, the attorneys present, even Mr. Settle, it seemed like an eternity.

Q. After going back into the apartment, how long did you stay?
A. About fifteen minutes.
Q. And then you left the apartment?
A. Yes, I did.
Q. About what time was this?
A. It could have been about six o'clock?
Q. Could it have been earlier?
A. It could have.
Q. Could it have been later?
A. It could have.
Q. When these people were put in the car, did they walk to the car?
A. Yes, they did.
Q. And this man, you say, walked each person to the car. Is that correct?
A. Yes, it is.
Q. Their feet were not bound in any way?
A. No.
Q. Now this first man, how would you describe his build?
A. Medium.
Q. Medium?
A. Five feet nine, or maybe six feet. I can't really judge size. I can't even judge your size.
Q. And this first man was put in the backseat of the car?
A. He opened the passenger side, on the rear side, and pushed the first man into the car.

Q. Did he leave the car door open?
A. He left the door open.
Q. The passenger door. In the rear seat?
A. Yes.
Q. And then he went back into the apartment?
A. Yes, he did.
Q. Could you tell if the apartment door was closed, or not?
A. I wasn't paying any attention.
Q. You weren't paying attention? Are you telling us that you were paying so much attention to other things—?
A. There was so much going on around the car that I didn't pay attention to the door.
Q. Did you see him go in the door?
A. Yes, I did. And I saw him come out with another person.
Q. The second man that he got. What was his build?
A. Medium build. A little shorter. A little shabbier.

The questions continued. On and on, with Mr. Settle repeating the witness's answers nearly every time. And then they argued about whether or not the witness described the second man as stocky in the preliminary hearing. In fact, Mr. Settle read the original statement aloud and added "et cetera, et cetera, et cetera."

With that Ron Fields stood up and objected. "Your Honor, make him read the whole thing."

Mr. Settle glared at his opponent. The paper shook a little as he read aloud the rest of the statement: "Then he run back into the apartment and got a stocky man, this guy resists, and turns and twisted from side to side.'"

The rest of the testimony was as testy as ever between Mr. Settle and the witness. At the end of the testimony, a newspaper reporter found it extremely difficult to transcribe for his articles just exactly what had been the testimony of the witness who claimed (in an exhausting amount of words exchanged between the defense council and witness for the prosecution) to have seen a man put two men into the back of a blue sedan. They appeared to have their hands behind their backs. A woman was led out of the apartment last, and she was crying while the man had his arm around her neck. She was put in the front seat. The man ran back in the apartment and carried out a paper sack clutched under his arm. He put the sack between him and the girl in the front seat, and they drove off.

If Mr. Settle planned for the jury to see that the eyewitness was not believable, he may have accomplished what he set out to do. But, in so doing, he drew out the testimony such an agonizingly long time that he might have lost the jury one quarter of the way in.

CHAPTER TWENTY-FOUR

Testimony continued with the arrest of Thomas Simmons, his trip to Fort Smith, the examination of his vehicle, and his subsequent arrest.

John Settle tried to prove that Simmons's car had been searched without first acquiring a warrant, but Ron Fields produced a form signed by Simmons that gave police permission to search it.

The discovery of the bodies the evening that Simmons was arrested was handled with care by both the prosecutor and the defense attorney. Neither wanted to offend the victims' families or the members of the jury by getting too graphic with the details. Photographs were shown of the bodies in the tire, but they were not crystal clear, and thus not too hard for people to look at. Fields and Settle had already agreed not to show the gruesome ones to the jury, so as not to inflame the jury toward either side.

Prosecutor Fields called Don Taylor, an officer with the Arkansas State Police, to ask him questions about the discovery of Larry Price at Clear Creek Park. He held a topographical map of the area for Taylor to see and point to a certain spot when answering his questions.

Q. Approximately where was Larry Price located?

A. (Pointing to the map) He was located in this picnic area. Right down from a picnic table.

Q. (Pointing to the map) Is this a close-up picture?

A. Yes. Just over on the creek bank, from the picnic table, or from this drive, here.

Q. How was Larry Price situated? When you found him?

A. He was lying on his back, with his head down. He had one arm extended down toward the water. He was almost into the water. There was a root there that was holding his shoulder, but his head was resting . . . that was keeping him from going into the water. Also his left foot had hung a vine that was holding him some.

Q. Okay. Was he . . . Mr. Price visible from the road when you first pulled up?

A. No.

Q. How high were the sides of the ditch?

A. I didn't measure them. I would estimate they were six or eight feet.

Q. Can you give us an idea of the angle that the sides sloped?

A. Almost straight down.

Q. Straight up and down?

A. Yes.

Q. I notice in this picture there was water in the ditch?

A. Yes, sir.

Q. How wide was the ditch, about?

A. It was almost ten feet.

Q. On this photograph (pointing to another map) there are two earthen dams. Were those there at the time?

A. No. We placed those in there and pumped out the water.

Q. Why was that done?
A. We were looking for the officer's gun and his badge and any personal effects of the victims. The victims' billfolds were missing.
Q. Were any of those personal effects of the officer ever found?
A. No, sir.
Q. Okay. To your knowledge, have any of the effects of the victims been found?
A. No, sir. They haven't.

Fields finished questioning Taylor, and he turned the witness over to John Settle.

Settle asked Don Taylor, "Were any footprints taken of the area?"

"There was a footprint just to the east of where there was a trail in the leaves, where there was a small trail that come around—there is a log—a wheel stop, I guess to keep the traffic from going off. There was a footprint just east of the log stop there."

"Were there any comparisons made? Against Simmons's footprints?

"No, the plaster footprints weren't any good. Too many leaves."

Scheduling witnesses and estimating the number of minutes each would be questioned by both sides was a difficult job. Lawyers had to rush around, making sure that a certain witness would still be available if the schedule got all messed up. And if somebody got sick several different times, like Leona Powell did, and didn't show at the right time or even the correct day, everybody had to scramble.

In one instance, John Settle couldn't contact a man from Oklahoma Gas & Electric to ask him to appear two hours earlier than he was scheduled. In the middle of court proceedings, Settle asked if he could approach the bench.

"Judge, have you tried to call the gas company lately? The telephone is always busy."

The pistol found beneath the bodies in the tractor tires led to the testimony of Neal "Squeeb" Bryant, who dated Thomas Simmons's sister. Thomas's brother, Frank Simmons, lived in a rental house across the road from Squeeb.

The police found five empty cartridges in the gun that had once belonged to Squeeb. And there was an attempt to destroy the serial numbers on the gun, but the numbers were still legible and matched the records that Buster Brown's General Store in Fort Smith kept on the gun at the time Squeeb bought it.

Perhaps Squeeb gave the pistol to Leona. Her daughter, Vicki, said they once had a peeping Tom, and Squeeb gave it to her mother. Vicki also said her mother later sold the pistol.

But Squeeb said he lost his pistol while Thomas Simmons was in prison.

He said he lost his .38 caliber Colt (he described it as "real pretty") during a squirrel hunt. He subsequently reported it stolen to the Crawford County Sheriff's Office on the twelfth of December in 1976.

But just because he reported it stolen didn't mean it really was.

His testimony was comical. He told all about the squirrel hunt and the supplies he bought here and there to take up with him to his camp up by Lee Creek. He named his friends, the good ole boys who went with him. The card games they played. How he camped out in his truck.

He said that when he was leaving to come home, he had a flat tire on a "mighty rough road," really more like a trail. The gun must have slipped out of its holster when he stopped to change the tire. When he reached his home and was unpacking, he realized he had lost his pistol. He turned right around and went back, even though he was mighty tired.

But Squeeb had been interviewed on the tenth of January by Don Taylor of the Arkansas State Police. In that interview, he told Taylor that he had originally bought the gun because he'd been having some trouble with some people while he was deer hunting. He also stated that someone had stolen the gun out of his pickup while he was deer hunting and he'd reported it missing to the Van Buren Police about three years earlier. He also said he couldn't remember if he'd ever loaned it to Leona or not. He offered to take a lie detector test.

He took one but failed it.

Of course, the defense wanted to put a doubt in the jury's mind about Squeeb. According to ballistic experts, his gun was similar to the kind that fired the bullets that killed the three in the bloody bottoms of Kibler and the body found at Clear Creek.

But Squeeb was in Mississippi on a hunting trip with some other guys, who all testified that he was with them during the times in which the kidnappings and the murders took place.

There were some who wondered if good ole boys would lie for a friend.

Blood experts testified that no blood was found on Simmons's clothes. But if Simmons's sister, Leona, washed his clothes the night of the fifth of January, no blood would have been on his clothes when he was arrested on the sixth of January.

A hair found on Larry Price's sock was consistent with samples of hair taken from Thomas Simmons. A hair found on Ray Tate's undershirt was consistent with samples of hair taken from Thomas Simmons.

A limb hair of African-American origin was found in fingernail clippings from Ray Tate, but the hair expert agreed that Tate could have picked up the hair as he was thrown on the floorboard of his car. The car was often used to transfer black men, as well as other races, who had been arrested and were transported to jail in that same car.

Those at the autopsy who removed Jawana's clothes said her panty hose were on backward, and the belt around her had not been put through all the belt loops on her slacks. The semen found in the vagina of Jawana Price was blood type O—which Simmons was, but her husband was not.

Match books found in Simmons's car were the brand name of Good Value. The same brand of matches were found next to Simmons's bed. The same brand of matches were found in the detective's car.

Did Detective Tate smoke? He smoked Vantage cigarettes. It was possible that Good Value matches were popular because they were sold in Safeway stores, and it was conceivable that Ray Tate could have also used Good Value matches. But the matches Ray Tate used had the logo "Beware of Greek Gods" stamped on the cover.

Garrick Feldman, the publisher of *The Press Argus,* was not the kind of guy who wrote his editorials to please his readers or to curry favor with the local police. In fact, he liked to stir things up. His editorial that ran during the first of the trial was titled "Murder of the Month" because the murder trial of Eugene Perry—the man who was convicted of the murder of Kenneth Staton and his daughter Suzanne Ware—had taken place the month before. Perry's partner, Richard Anderson, would be tried after the Simmons trial.

The murder trials were putting a huge dent in Crawford County's treasury. The sheriff had to ask for more money to run his department. He reported that the Perry trial had cost the county ten thousand dollars, counting everything and everyone involved with preparing for and conducting the actual trial. Jurors had to be paid and sometimes fed.

Feldman wrote that some of the reporters who sat in on the trial were disappointed that they didn't feel any electricity or a crisp atmosphere in the courtroom. The murder trial of a man who killed a cop and three other people should be more exciting.

Feldman explained, "the lawyers weren't that interesting." His column read, "This trial is not dazzling because neither of the lawyers involved are dazzling in the courtroom." He opined that the lawyers tended to be bland, at times sounding like law students in a mock trial.

Feldman also reported that, "Simmons's complexion changed daily as he sat quietly in a brown two-piece suit. His coloring turned yellow as each day progressed, and close to the end of the trial, he looked like a shriveled lemon."

CHAPTER TWENTY-FIVE

Character witnesses were called in Thomas Simmons's behalf.

A neighbor, Larry Lynn, testified that he seemed like a good man and seemed to be of help to his sister and the children.

A Methodist minister testified for him, even though he didn't know him well because Simmons had only attended his church a few times. The minister did not believe in the death penalty, which may have been the reason for his testimony.

A college teacher, a Catholic nun who taught classes to prisoners at Leavenworth, came to testify for Simmons.

Her testimony was deemed to be powerful by those who listened to the trial and later read the trial transcript.

John Settle asked the following questions of his defense witness.

Q. State your name, please.

A. Sister Celine Carrigan.

Q. And you are a Sister?

A. Yes. Benedictine.

Q. Are you employed at the present time?

A. I am instructor of English at Benedictine College in Hutchinson, Kansas.

Q. What sort of courses do you teach?
A. I teach writing, freshman composition, upper division English, British romantic literature, and Shakespeare.
Q. Have you taught prior to teaching at Benedictine College?
A. Yes, I taught sixteen years in the upper metropolitan area of Kansas City.
Q. In the course of your employment at Benedictine College, did you also teach classes at Leavenworth prison?
A. I taught English classes for the college.
Q. Was Tom Simmons enrolled in some of those classes?
A. Yes. He was enrolled in English, composition, and introduction to literature.
Q. Were those the only courses he was taking?
A. I believe he took Spanish, an accounting class, and an econ class.
Q. Besides those classes?
A. He was enrolled in a computer programming course. I believe that went during the day hours, and then it was customary that the men would take the college courses in the evening between six and nine o'clock. I know that Thomas Simmons was enrolled in that computing course. I was there for their graduation when he won an award for excellence. Only one or two got that award for the spring semester. I also believe he was taking correspondence classes through the University of Kansas.
Q. Tell me about Tom as a student.
A. I knew right away that he was going to make the highest grades. I don't think he missed a class. He

> was very interested and helpful to other students who were having difficulty in the classes.
> Q. Did he show a desire to learn and try to improve himself?
> A. That is my overall remembrance, that he definitely wanted to learn. He asked me a year ago, when I was not teaching him, if I would write a letter for him to the parole board. I told him I'd be happy to.

When Ron Fields was given the chance to question Sister Celine, he was, of course, very respectful. He asked the Sister if taking classes would be more interesting to prisoners, than, say, working in the prison kitchen.

And, he asked, wouldn't a prisoner try to curry favors from his teacher, especially if the teacher rewarded his hard work with As?

He also asked Sister Celine if her letter to the parole board was successful.

"No," she answered. "Not at that time."

Thomas Simmons listened to his teacher with a huge lump in his throat. She had always been kind to him. In fact, it was compliments she gave him in class, in front of other students, that made him study harder and earn top grades. Nobody, ever, had been as kind to him as his dear friend Sister Celine.

When she left the stand, Sister Celine looked at Tom and smiled.

He mouthed the words, "Thank you."

Leona Powell, bless her heart, was subpoenaed three times to testify in the trial of her brother. At each scheduled time, she either got sick and fell, couldn't climb the stairs at the court house, or was under a physician's care. Of course, by not showing up at the scheduled times, she royally inconvenienced everyone. Finally, with Judge Holland's approval, both sides decided to present the jury with a Stipulation of Facts, a legal document that substituted a written statement of a witness instead of the witness testifying in person at a trial.

Many folks wondered: What is she afraid of?

The statement began, "That Leona Powell lives in Kibler, Arkansas. That the phone number that the Alma exchange lists in the name of Ron Simmons, number 632-4879, is located in her home, and that Ron Simmons, a brother, pays for the bill. That on the night of January fifth, 1981, around nine o'clock, Thomas Simmons called her residence and stated that he needed a ride home from the Speedy Mart located at I-40 and Highway 59, and that she and her daughter went and picked him up at that location. That on the ride home, Thomas Simmons stated to her that his car was at Central Mall in Fort Smith, Arkansas. That when asked if he wanted to go get his car then, he stated that he had a headache and wished to be taken to the residence where he was living at the time. Leona Powell went to Central Mall parking lot with the daughter and located Thomas Simmons's 1975 yellow Toyota parked near the Mall Trio Theater's entrance.

"That Thomas Simmons never stated to Leona Powell that he had any kind of accident, nor did she know that he had not gone to work on Monday, January fifth, as scheduled."

Leona Powell would further testify, "that a niece of Thomas Simmons was employed at J. C. Penney's in Central Mall and that her normal work hours were twelve in the afternoon until nine that night. That after Simmons's arrest, he told Leona Powell that the reason he had left his car at Central Mall parking lot was for the niece to pick it up and drive it home. That he did not take the car keys in to her."

Leona Powell signed the notarized statement and soon after moved out of Kibler to an unknown address.

Obviously, skilled lawyers questioning a woman in the murder trial of her brother would rather have her sitting in a witness chair in front of a jury, under the watchful eye of a judge sitting at a desk above her. The United States of America's flag sits on one side and the Arkansas flag sits on the other. She would have to put her right hand on the Bible and swear to tell the truth, and nothing but the truth.

Perhaps she could be tricked and say something she didn't mean to say. Perhaps she could become so flustered she would say something that would prove her brother killed four people. Perhaps she'd even implicate his accomplice. Or two or three.

But she was allowed to dictate a statement and never had to speak a word.

Thomas Simmons chose not to testify at all. Judge Holland instructed the jurors to not draw any conclusions about innocence or guilt concerning this decision. It was Simmons's right not to testify at his trial.

CHAPTER TWENTY-SIX

Judge Holland read his instructions to the jury, which must have made a few of the jurors look aghast since the instructions seemed complicated, but they would be able to take a copy of the instructions with them when they began deliberating the case.

Ron Fields was first with his closing statement. He explained some of Judge Holland's instructions. He wanted them to use their common sense.

"You aren't required to set aside your common knowledge when you listened to the technicalities of the case." He looked each juror in the eye. "Our system is predicated on twelve people using their common sense they have accumulated in their life to make these decisions."

He continued, trying to explain the way the jury system worked.

"If after an impartial consideration of all the evidence, and a juror is satisfied beyond a reasonable doubt, he must then vote the way he or she sees fit."

The state contended that Thomas Simmons was guilty of capital murder. And that the four people killed—Larry Price, Jawana Price, Ray Tate, and Holly Gentry—were all kidnapped and, in the course of that crime, were murdered. They were robbed of their possessions. Tate had his badge taken and his gun stolen out of its holster. His billfold was also missing, and the others' billfolds and purse were never found. Jawana was raped. Ray Tate was murdered in the line of duty.

Fields said four people were killed by someone who showed extreme indifference to human life. And that someone was Thomas Simmons.

"Larry Price didn't pick up his wife for lunch, he didn't show up for work, and he was found in Clear Creek Park. He didn't do all these things for the heck of it. He was kidnapped and ended up dead—with his jacket pulled up behind his neck—by a bullet shot into the back of his head."

Fields explained that Jawana was killed in much the same way as her husband. Her coat was pulled up on her neck, and then she too was shot in the back of the head, exactly the way Holly Gentry and Ray Tate were. But before that she suffered the indignity of rape.

Fields went over the circumstantial evidence.

"Keep in mind that circumstantial evidence is very, very important. Let's see what we know about the defendant's whereabouts that day.

"First of all, he didn't show up for work that morning because his foreman, Jim Pence, said he didn't. He said he'd had an accident, but he never mentioned an accident to his sister or anyone else.

"The second thing we know is that he was over here in Van Buren at the Industrial Park branch bank, which is right down the road that you go on to where the first murder site is at Clear Creek Park. We know about the time because the bank clerk testified it was at ten o'clock when he deposited that check number 209 that is in evidence.

"And where was he before that? We know that Ernie Kremers saw him that morning, looking at the car with Larry Price around eight or eight thirty.

"And we've got the statement that Jawana Price gave the detectives with a description of the man who was with her husband in their apartment when she left at eight forty to go to work.

"The lady at Baldor said the man who called in said Larry Price wouldn't be at work that day. She said she recognized the voice as not belonging to Larry Price. The voice was somebody between thirty-five or forty years old. And all of us know that we can usually judge a person's voice and tell how old they are. We don't have to be a voice expert to do that.

"Where is the next place we can place him? In the parking lot at Phoenix Village Mall around four or four thirty. He's sitting in his yellow 1975 Toyota that is parked so close to Jawana's car that it alarmed Don Seaton, the custodian, while he was out picking up trash. Seaton took down the license number IFS 053. And keep in mind, Simmons knew about the time she got off work, and he would have gotten her if she hadn't gone with Holly Gentry, who parked his truck on the opposite side of the mall.

"We've got a cab driver who can't positively say it was Simmons, but it was someone who fit his description, that he picked up at Osco Drug in Central Mall and delivered him to 710 North Forty-Eighth Street. And remember the Ford LTD that was for sale was found at Central Mall near where Simmons left his yellow Toyota and asked his sister to get for him around ten or eleven that night. He couldn't go, he said, because he had a headache. I bet he did have a headache. He'd killed four people that day.

"Back up a little bit to nine thirty, when he entered the Speedy Mart that's almost next door to the Union 76 truck stop where Detective Tate's car was found. He asked the clerk if he could get a taxi that time of night. She told him she doubted it. So he is forced to call his sister to come and get him. He knows his little yellow car needs to be picked up, but he doesn't want to be seen anywhere near Central Mall, so he makes his sister go.

"Just like his teacher testified, 'he is very thorough in his work.'"

Fields next talked about the significance of the testimony of James Davis, who testified that he saw three people ushered out of the Price apartment into a plain Ford sedan. One by one, two men with their hands behind their backs were pushed into the backseat of the car. Since he couldn't see their heads, he assumed they were on the floor board. And a woman, who looked like she was crying, got into the passenger side of the car.

Fields looked directly at each one of the jurors. "Why didn't the woman try to run away? She was terrified, that's why. And maybe the man told her he would take her to her husband? We don't know. We can only surmise."

Of course, Thomas Simmons made a huge mistake in trying to retrieve the check from the bank. And the prosecutor, minute by minute, went over that morning of the sixth of January.

"What were the odds," he asked, "that the wife of a policeman who worked at Citizens Bank in the Cloverleaf Shopping Center would recognize the name of the man who signed the check as belonging to the person who was kidnapped?"

She was one smart policeman's wife to look out the window and get the license plate number on a little yellow Toyota.

Next, Fields reminded the jury that when Simmons was arrested, he had one hundred and forty four dollars in his billfold. That was quite a lot of money for a man who was broke the day before. Fields suggested that the money, minus the fifty he took out of the bogus check he'd deposited, came from the victims since their billfolds were never found.

The jury was asked to consider the gun that was found under the bodies in the bloody Kibler bottoms. The bullets were so mangled from passing through the victims' heads that the experts could only say that they resembled ones that would come from the .38 Colt found in the grave. The very same gun that Squeeb Bryant claimed was stolen years earlier.

In his final summation, Fields asked the jury to look at the aerial photographs made of the area in which the bodies were found.

"Could you pick a more desolate spot to hide bodies? There's just nothing around there. One house a quarter of a mile away and then the paved road is way up the road. No way in the world could you go to the bottoms at night and find your way around. You know what those are like. Hot, pitch-black they are at night. And yet, where Larry Price was found over at Clear Creek Park, you can go through the bottoms to get there, or you can go right down Kibler Road. And who would know that area better than somebody that's been living there?"

Fields pointed to a big topographical map that was facing the jury. "And where does Simmons live?" he asked, pointing with a ruler. "Right in the middle of where these two sites are.

"And keep in mind that the bodies were hid fairly well. With the intensive, intensive search, Larry Price wasn't found for two days, and then by someone who just stumbled onto him. The other three wouldn't have been found if the McClures hadn't happened to be out there by that tractor tire. Look at the photographs of the tractor tire and see how carefully they were hidden. You really can't even tell that there are bodies hidden in that tractor tire in the big, blow-up photograph unless you look very hard."

The prosecutor paused, took a breath. His shoulders drooped, like someone who's worked very hard plowing a field or digging ditches or laying concrete. Preparing a case in which four people were killed and then presenting it to a jury for consideration was a very tough job, both mentally and physically.

"Ladies and gentlemen, I submit to you that when you have examined the evidence, have gone through it very carefully, you will agree, as we have, that the same person committed all four murders, and that that person is Thomas W. Simmons. Thank you."

Judge Holland then asked the jury to give their attention to Mr. Settle for the defendant.

John Settle opened his closing remarks with the big Million Dollar Question. Where was Larry Price when Tom Simmons was running around all day between Fort Smith and Van Buren? He always called his client Tom Simmons because it seemed more personal.

Settle also reminded the jury that the state's medical examiner said that Larry Price probably died after the other three were murdered. Dr. Malak told the jury that Larry Price was lying flat on his back after he died. But, when his body was found, at least four hours after he was killed, the body was lying almost straight up, hanging down an embankment to a creek. That proved the body was moved.

Settle argued that this question on its own demolished the theory that one man alone committed four murders.

Settle reminded the jury that no fingerprints of his client were found. Only a spot of blood was found on the blue pants he was wearing, and that blood was type O, which was the same blood type of most of the people who lived in his house—and about another billion people.

And the star witness? James Davis couldn't decide if he saw certain events at the Glenn-Holly Apartment Complex at five o'clock or five thirty or six o'clock or six thirty. And he sure couldn't tell what anyone looked like or the kind of clothes they were wearing.

If Michelle McClure heard noises between seven and eight out in the spinach fields, then the murderer would have blood on his clothes from the actual murders and the blood from the bodies as they were tossed into the tractor tires. But the girl at Speedy Mart saw no blood on Simmons when he arrived at the store around nine to inquire about taxi service.

"They weren't bloody, muddy, wet, dirty or anything else," Settle opined loudly.

"And what about the African-American hair found among the fingernail clippings of Detective Ray Tate? Did that come from an African-American during a struggle? He could very well be the man who was involved in the murders."

The state wanted the jury to think Jawana was raped because her panty hose were inside out and her belt had missed a loop. And did the jury really think that Jawana took off her clothes to be raped and then put them back on again? And where did he rape her? In the police unit belonging to Ray Tate? If so, wouldn't there be evidence of rape occurring in the car's front or backseat? Or did he rape her on the muddy ground? And if so, wouldn't her body would be muddy and his clothes as well? There were no bruises or lacerations on her private parts.

And if Larry Price was shot and killed last with a .38 Colt pistol, then how did the gun wind up beneath the bodies in the tire?

And did the Good Value matchbooks really prove anything? Those were sold at lots of grocery stores in Arkansas. Probably Oklahoma and Missouri also.

Settle said in closing, "Ladies and gentlemen, I told you in the beginning that there were a lot of questions involved in this matter. I told you there were a lot of questions. I told you I would not be able to answer them for you.

"After all the evidence has been presented to you, not only do these questions remain, but new questions have been raised. These questions are what I would call doubts, reasonable doubts. They have not been resolved. Ladies and gentlemen, you must find Tom Simmons not guilty. Thank you."

The prosecutor was allowed to give his rebuttal to the closing statement made by the defendant's attorney.

Ron Fields didn't speak long. He knew the jury was tired. He didn't want to bore them by going over the same material again and again. He hit a few points raised by Settle concerning blood spots and fingerprints missing on a gun that lay at the bottom of a muddy grave under cold and wet conditions.

Judge Holland gave more instructions to the jury after it was decided by both attorneys and the judge that the group would eat their lunch after hearing the instructions, and when they returned, they would begin deliberating the verdict.

The Crawford County Sheriff, Trellon Ball, took fourteen jurors to lunch at the Farmers' Co-Op on Industrial Park Road, the road that led to Kibler. There were no ulterior motives in choosing the Co-Op. It was the best place to eat in town. There was a good noon buffet, and there was plenty of room to accommodate a large group.

When the group returned, full and not a bit sleepy, they entered the jury room at exactly one o'clock. The two alternates were thanked and dismissed.

The jury returned at three forty-five with a verdict.

They found Thomas Simmons guilty of capital murder for each of the four victims: Larry Price, Jawana Price, Holly Gentry, and Detective Ray Tate.

The jury was individually polled at the request of John Settle. All twelve jurors had to agree to the guilty verdict, and they each did, one by one.

The jury was not free to go. Their next decision was to decide upon the punishment for Thomas Simmons.

Judge Holland gave more instructions, telling the jury that this next deliberation would be the hardest.

"Unfortunately," he said, "Arkansas is one of the states that requires the jury to set the punishment in a capital murder trial."

Once again, each side pled its case.

Ron Fields was first. "Ladies and gentlemen, as the judge has told you, in a few minutes you will retire to deliberate the sentence in this case. That is going to be an unpleasant task. It is. I want you to keep in mind a couple of very important points and that is that there are four reasons why we talk about sentencing someone to anything in the criminal justice system. The first reason is obviously punishment. We punish people for what they have done.

"The second reason is rehabilitation. We always like to think in terms of when we rehabilitate this person and make him a safe, sane, productive member of society.

"The third thing is we punish people as a means of deterring them and making certain that this person, if he is punished enough, would not commit this crime again or any other crime. And the fourth reason is to be a deterrent to others."

He reminded the jury that Simmons was already convicted in August of 1971 for kidnapping a young man, seriously wounding him, and leaving him for dead under a pile of leaves in a rural area outside of Little Rock. Miraculously, the young man survived by dragging himself to a farmhouse and asking for help. He healed well enough to testify in court, and Simmons received forty-five years in prison. But he got out on parole in eight years. He was sent right after that to the federal pen in Leavenworth for assaulting an FBI agent, forcibly taking his gun, and stealing his car at approximately the same time he kidnapped the young man. He fooled everybody and was paroled in 1980, and here he was, again, but this time for kidnapping and murder.

People like Thomas Simmons were what gave rehabilitation a bad name.

"You know there was a witness in the first kidnapping case because the guy didn't die," Fields said, looking intently at each juror. "There weren't any four witnesses here today. Ray Tate, Jawana Price, Larry Price, and Holly Gentry weren't here to testify in this trial. I am submitting to you for these reasons we need to impose the death penalty in this case.

"It is a very, very harsh sentence. Is it a deterrent to others? Well, let's think for a second. Deterrent means to cause someone to avoid something because of fear. What deterrent does Simmons fear the most? The death penalty or life in prison?

"I'm sympathetic to the victims' families. I'm sympathetic to the defendant's family. I submit to you that the defendant had a responsibility to his family way before this happened. He failed them over and over.

"Simmons is the one that determined his own punishment the day he killed those four people out in Kibler and Clear Creek Park.

"The conscience of the community is the jury system. You are the twelve people in this entire community, in this entire county, who can speak and speak out on what you feel about this type of crime. It is a heavy burden, but it is one that must be shouldered. I'm asking you for the death penalty in this case. You must be the conscience of your community."

John Settle was "loaded for bear," as they say in Crawford County and other parts of Arkansas.

"Ladies and gentlemen, you have found Tom Simmons guilty of these offenses, so you think he was involved in this. Ladies and gentlemen, I submit to you that this case has a lot of questions. It is a very open case. I will tell you that we are not going to deny his record, but I would assert and I would tell you he had much to live for.

"In this type of case, it is understandable why a jury or a community would feel anger in this type of situation, but I tell you there's far more involved in this case than Tom Simmons.

"Some argue that the death penalty is a deterrent. I would say that that is too speculative to say. You cannot make that determination, and certainly, nobody has—what has been presented does not support that conclusion.

"Two possible sentences in this type of case, both extremely harsh. That is life without parole. Life without parole. For some, it is more than death itself.

"The family of Tom Simmons knows exactly what the families of the victims are going through. Their families have been deprived as well. They have been deprived of someone they love. It is a very difficult thing for everyone.

"Ladies and gentlemen, Tom Simmons has the capacity to love, the capacity to be loved, and I would tell you that I feel any person who has that ability is a human being. For you who vote for death in this case means that each one of you, each one of you will stand up and say, 'Yes, I want him to die, and yes, I will kill him.'"

Settle closed with telling the jury that he didn't think they were so convinced in their own minds that was what they wanted. That was what was needed.

Then, after a long pause, he thanked the jury.

The defendant's lawyer had barely sat down before the prosecutor stood up. He could barely contain himself. He was disgusted by John Settle laying a guilt trip on the jury members.

"Just a couple of comments on that, ladies and gentlemen. I want you to keep in mind that what you are doing won't be the final word. The final word happened out there in that field that day with those three people and the one at Clear Creek. At that time, the defendant was the one that selected what he was going to do out there that day. None of us had that responsibility. There is not a one of you that wouldn't have done all you could to prevent this, just like all those four people would have.

"You know, the defendant in every case is entitled to a fair trial, and you know, I asked you that question myself every time in *voir dire*, 'Would you give the defendant a fair trial because he is entitled to one, but that is all he is entitled to. He is not entitled to have sympathy for him or his family or anything like that to sway you in this case.'

"A fair trial in a capital murder case means that the State has got to have twenty-four votes. Twenty-four votes. There has to be twelve on guilty or innocence; there's got to be twelve on the capital penalty phase. Twenty-four to zero. What can be more fair to the defendant?"

CHAPTER TWENTY-SEVEN

The jury left at five forty p.m.to decide the punishment for Thomas Simmons.

They returned at seven ten.

Their unanimous verdict was death by electrocution.

The judge asked Simmons if he had anything to say.

"I do," he said. "I came here in this very courtroom on August eighth and said I was innocent. I am still innocent."

The judge thanked the jury and said they were free to go.

The trial had begun on the fifth of August, 1981. Eight months to the day after four people were killed in the peaceful little community of Kibler.

The trial ended on the nineteenth of August, 1981.

A notice of appeal was filed on September seventeenth, 1981.

At one time, in the Arkansas prison, Thomas Simmons was a cellmate of Eugene Perry, who was found guilty of the murder of Kenneth Staton and his daughter Suzanne Staton Ware during a

Farm field where bodies were found almost forty years ago.
Note bare spot that depict the location of the bodies.

robbery of their jewelry store in Van Buren, Arkansas, on September the tenth, 1980.

The Crawford County jury had given him the death sentence also, so both men waited out their appeal processes at the same time while in prison on death row.

Those two crimes were both successfully prosecuted by Ron Fields.

Another murder took place in Van Buren on the eighteenth of May, 1981. A prominent woman, Ruie Ann Park, a one-time owner of *The Press Argus* newspaper, was found bludgeoned to death in her mansion on top of Logtown Hill. The murderer entered a guilty plea and therefore was not prosecuted by Ron Fields.

These three different murder cases took place in a period of only nine months. All in Crawford County, Arkansas.

When Thomas Simmons's appeals were all denied, he decided he didn't want to subject his family to the newspaper and television coverage that would inevitably accompany his execution. Leona and the girls had suffered enough because of him. He thought he'd have the last laugh at the criminal justice system of Arkansas. He wrapped himself in a blanket and slit his throat with a knife he fashioned out of a piece of metal. He left this world on New Year's Eve, ten years after he'd been sentenced to death.

Van Buren has been described as a sleepy little river town.

The Kibler bottoms was farmland nourished by the Arkansas River, land that some families owned for generation after generation. From this land, produce grew and fed families in Arkansas,

Oklahoma, Missouri, Texas, and beyond. Cattle grazed on green grasses that provided hamburgers and T-bone steaks. Chicken farmers signed contracts with big companies like Tyson and built their chicken houses on land that wasn't much good for anything else.

For a long time, people had a hard time sleeping, wondering what else was going to happen. But bit by bit, the landscape changed. Families moved. New families moved in. Before long, children were allowed to play outdoors at night and chase fireflies and put them in Mason jars. Parents sat outside in lawn chairs and swatted mosquitoes.

Occasionally, someone might bring up the murders that happened down in the bottoms.

AUTHOR'S NOTES

My research for this book was through conversations with people who knew people who remembered certain things, but couldn't remember other things. I read newspaper articles and, most importantly, I had the transcript of the trial, which I used to tell the story of the senseless murders of four people and the police investigations that brought Thomas Simmons to stand trial and be convicted.

In those days, the police checked for fingerprints by dusting a black powder over surfaces. If a print appeared, then plain old Scotch tape was laid over the print and then lifted up and placed on a three-by-five white card. Hardly a real scientific way of gathering prints. DNA testing was unheard of then, and forensic testing was not around. If there had been the scientific methods of today to solve crimes, then perhaps we'd know the real story of the cold-blooded murders that happened in the Kibler Bottoms.

It's an emotional tug on my heart to sit at a computer and tell the stories of people being murdered. I have tried to treat each victim with a tender hand, and in all cases, I've thought about the families who might be reading my books. I didn't want to unnecessarily harm anyone, but yet, I wanted to tell a true story, in the way I understood it to be true.

I was also told some pretty wild tales about happenings on that tragic day on the fifth of January, 1981, and the days thereafter. Those tales did not jive with the court transcript of sworn witnesses, so I left them out of the book. What I did discover, however, is that my own take on what occurred was different than what the state prosecutor was able to use in court. He was only concerned with convicting Thomas Simmons, the job that was given to him. My take on the events of those days is my own personal opinion, but I share it with you here at the end because it helps to make more sense of the facts that are known.

Here's what I think happened.

On Saturday, the third of January, Thomas Simmons left his sister's home in Kibler and drove to Fort Smith to check out the car advertised in the newspaper that was for sale at 710 North Forty-Eighth Street. He'd seen the ad in the paper a few days earlier. It sounded like a real nice car, and he knew a man I'll call "John" who bought stolen cars. He thought if he stole it, he could sell it for enough money to pay his tuition and books at Westark Community College, where he had already registered but not paid the tuition.

I think he tried to be a good brother to his sister and a good father to his daughter. But his job was hard, and he needed fast money to go to college. He had this crazy idea that he could one day make his family proud of him. Going to college was his ticket out of crime. He'd been good at computer work. He found that out in prison when he was able to take college courses.

But the man selling the car was out of town, and a man who lived at the apartment complex told him to come back on Monday, the day that would be Simmons's first day back at work after a long two weeks of being off work. He really needed to get back to work. He barely had enough money to put gas in his car, but he desperately wanted to get that Ford LTD.

The following Monday morning, Simmons dressed for work in heavy clothes because he worked outside. His sister cooked his breakfast, and he left her home in Kibler about five thirty. He didn't tell his sister he wasn't going to work, but he had no plans of such. He called Arkhola Sand and Gravel and said he wouldn't be in because he'd had a wreck.

He drove across the Arkansas River Bridge and stopped at Yeager's Liquor Store with his last little bit of money and bought a pint of gin courage. He then drove to the apartments and saw that the Ford LTD was still parked in the parking area with the "For Sale" sign still in place.

After knocking on the door, he was surprised when a young woman answered. He told her he was interested in buying the car that was advertised. Jawana said she'd have to wake her husband. She did not invite him in, just shut the door and left him out standing in the cold, which made him angry.

Simmons and Larry Price went on a test drive, and both returned to Larry's apartment, where Simmons again saw Jawana as she was leaving for work at eight forty. As he always did, Larry walked his wife to her car, and when he returned, Simmons was waiting for Larry with a gun he'd gotten from his sister's boyfriend, Neil "Squeeb" Bryant.

Simmons told Larry not to be alarmed. He just needed money real bad, and he wanted the car. The two or three swallows of gin from the bottle in his jacket pocket had given him courage, and his self-esteem went up enough to make him confident to pull this off. He'd already found John, who would buy the car for fifteen hundred dollars. That would be enough to pay his tuition and buy the college textbooks he'd need.

They left the apartment, with Larry driving the Ford LTD. Simmons rode on the passenger side and held the gun on him. Simmons directed Larry to drive to Clear Creek Park in Kibler, which was usually deserted on cold winter mornings. He walked Larry past the picnic area toward the creek and shot him in the back of his head. Left for dead, Larry valiantly tried to get up, but instead, he thrashed around to the edge of the creek and fell down the bank in an almost vertical position.

Around ten o'clock, Simmons stopped at the bank on Industrial Park Road, which is directly on the way from Kibler to Van Buren and then I-540 to Fort Smith. He was driving the stolen car, but nobody knew it was stolen at that time. He deposited a forged check on Larry's bank account for three hundred and fifty dollars, and then he withdrew two twenties and a ten. This was his undoing, and I can't figure out why he took such a chance. Criminals are not nearly as smart as they think they are. He was not a dumb man, so I suspect his liquid courage impaired his intellect.

Simmons then drove the Ford LTD to Central Mall Shopping Center and left the car near the Mall Trio Theater, where the transfer of the stolen car would later take place. He walked to Osco Drug and telephoned for a taxi to return him to the apartment at 710 North Forty-Eighth so he could get his yellow Toyota.

Around two thirty that afternoon, he called Baldor to say Larry Price wouldn't be in for work. He also called John, who was going to buy the stolen car, and told him to meet him at eight o'clock at Central Mall near the Mall Trio Theater.

Simmons was becoming more and more paranoid.

At four thirty, he drove to Phoenix Village Mall, and once he located Jawana's car, he parked next to it and waited for her to get off work. He knew what kind of car she drove because he had seen her leave for work that morning. His plan was to stop her in the parking lot and tell her that he'd take her to Larry. He had to kill her too, to keep her from identifying him.

When she didn't return to her car, he drove his little Toyota back to Central Mall and parked it near the mall theater.

He then walked to Osco Drug, which was close by, and called for a taxi. He was worried that someone from the apartment complex would recognize his car.

Around five thirty, the taxi delivered him to the Price apartment. He had stolen Larry's keys and billfold, so he opened the apartment door and waited for Jawana. He then called John and asked him to come pick him up at the apartment. To sweeten the deal, he told him that Jawana was a cute little thing.

Minutes later, John arrived, and they both waited on Jawana. Simmons told his friend he could screw her first.

When Jawana and Holly opened the apartment door, they were welcomed by two men, one carrying a gun. The bad guys were as surprised as Jawana and Holly were.

Simmons pushed Jawana on the couch and grabbed Holly by the arm. John found some heavy twine in a kitchen drawer and tied up Holly. Jawana made a break for the bedroom where the phone was, but Simmons grabbed her and tore the cord out of the phone. Screaming and crying, she was pulled back into the living room. She told the men that the police were coming, and they had better leave. Of course, they didn't believe her.

But Detective Ray Tate did arrive and knocked on the apartment door. When no one answered, he turned the doorknob and slowly pushed the door open. He was jumped and handcuffed with his own cuffs. John took the weapon out of Tate's holster.

Now Simmons and John both had guns. They discussed what to do with the threesome. Since Larry Price was already dead at Clear Creek Park, they decided to take the threesome there. Simmons promised John he could rape Jawana when they got there.

Ray Tate and Holly Gentry struggled valiantly. Simmons threatened to kill Jawana if they didn't get in the back floor board of the detective's car. The detective was sure he could get Holly untied once they were in the car, but he couldn't.

They drove to Van Buren, and then Simmons decided to take the threesome into the Kibler bottoms. Simmons was familiar with the area, having taken his daughter and her friends on rides through the bottoms. At dark, the deserted bottoms seemed the perfect spot for dumping three dead bodies.

I think Simmons shot both men in the back of the head while John raped Jawana on the hood of the car. Simmons then sodomized Jawana before killing her the same way he killed the men. And then they tossed the gun in and dumped all three bodies in a sunken junk pile of old tractor tires, diesel cans, and old irrigation pipes that just happened to be where they stopped.

They then drove Tate's vehicle to the Union 76 truck stop and parked it there. Simmons told John where the Ford LTD was parked in Central Mall and gave him the keys. They would meet the next night, at which time Simmons would get his money.

Simmons walked over to the Speedy Mart, used their restroom to wash up, and called his sister to come pick him up. John, who was on parole from the Oklahoma State Penitentiary in Muskogee and had spent most of his adult life stealing cars, went inside the Union 76 men's room. When he came out, he ordered a cup of coffee and a piece of cherry pie. He then called a buddy who lived up on Highway 59 and worked at a used tire store and asked him to come pick him up and take him over to Fort Smith where he left his car, which he'd stolen in another state. He'd left it parked at a QuikPik on Grand.

By the time John got to Central Mall to retrieve the Ford LTD and leave the stolen car he was driving, cops had surrounded the car so, of course, he didn't stop. The time was around ten thirty, and Detective Tate's car was found around an hour later.

I can't for the life of me figure out why there was no blood on Simmons. Perhaps pulling the back of a coat over the head prevents blood from spattering after someone is shot. Perhaps Simmons had a change of clothes.

I just know that four people were brutally murdered. I think Simmons did it or was part of it, but he needed help to dispose of the bodies. Dead bodies are indeed "dead weight."

I also don't believe the story of Simmons's suicide in jail.

Eugene Perry, who was sentenced to death in the Van Buren Staton Jewelry Robbery case, had bragged that he was part of the Dixie Mafia.

Perhaps Simmons had decided to tell the authorities who helped him.

Maybe the Dixie Mafia ordered Perry to kill Simmons to keep him quiet. They were cellmates. I don't believe a man could commit suicide by slitting his own throat. And even if he did, why would he wrap himself up in a blanket first? It seems much more logical that he was murdered in his cell.

I hesitated to write this book using the details as I saw them because they are, in the end, my own conclusions, not the facts presented at trial. I will leave it to you as the reader to decide which story makes the most sense. If I am correct in my assessment of the chain of events, these crimes are even more premeditated and cold-blooded than the sad story of needless rape and murder that was presented at trial.

This is the third true-crime novel I've written about murders that occurred in my hometown of Van Buren within a nine-month period of time. With each one, I felt a real connection to all the victims of these brutal murders, as well as to their families. And because of their stories, I've made lifelong friends whom I cherish.

– THE END –

But wait—there's more!

BLIND RAGE

A true story of sin, sex, and murder in a small Arkansas town. Who did it and why will shock you.

When Ruie Ann Park—a pillar of the Van Buren, Arkansas, community—was found beaten to death and lying in a pool of blood in her home, the police and local residents assumed the son was the murderer. But the years would uncover a more sinister story.

Until that night, the Park family seemed to have it all. For fifty years they owned and published the Press Argus newspaper. Hugh was well-connected politically, and his wife, Ruie Ann, was the local historian, journalist, and teacher. They had a brilliant son and a shy adopted daughter.

They built a beautiful home on top of Logtown Hill with a vista overlooking the Arkansas River, but their idyllic life ended with divorce. Ruie Ann stayed in the home, becoming more bitter and more demanding of the daughter who couldn't match up to her beloved son.

The son, Sam Hugh, had a promising legal career, but his fondness for young boys, alcohol, and drugs doomed what should have been a successful law practice in his hometown. The daughter, Linda, graduated from college, married an attorney, and moved away to a small town near Little Rock.

The police were baffled. Who was smart enough to hide all evidence and pass the lie detector test?

And who would want to bludgeon this mother to death?

CLOSING TIME

A true story of robbery and ruthless double murder that shook a small town.

Kenneth Staton was the well-respected owner of a jewelry store in Van Buren, Arkansas. Although crippled with rheumatoid arthritis and unable to walk without crutches, he had built his business through excellent watch repair work, fine quality jewelry sold at fair prices, and a dedication to his customers that surpassed all other merchants. He was the quintessential gentleman in all aspects of his life, and a beloved father.

Unknown to him, two men—a seasoned criminal with a propensity for violence and a younger man, handsome, but broke and with an obsessive thirst for alcohol—plotted to rob the jewelry store at closing time on September 10, 1980. The thugs had only met each other days before, and it was the younger one's first venture into armed robbery.

When Staton and his daughter Suzanne didn't show up for supper, his other two daughters became alarmed and went to the store. There they found the bodies of their father and youngest sister lying in pools of blood, gagged, hogtied, and shot twice in the head. Close to $100,000 dollars in diamonds and other jewelry had been stolen.

This senseless, bloody crime rocked the town of Van Buren and set its lawmen, sworn to find the killers, on a fiercely determined hunt that led from Rogers, Arkansas to Jacksonville, Florida, and all the way to Vancouver, Canada.

Seventeen years later, was justice served?

GET YOUR COPY TODAY AT

WWW.PEN-L.COM/CLOSINGTIME.HTML

AVAILABLE IN PRINT, KINDLE, AND AUDIO BOOK.

ACKNOWLEDGEMENTS

First of all, I want to thank Kristen Edwards with the Crawford County Circuit Clerk's Office in Van Buren for the valuable help in finding the transcript of the murder trial for Thomas Simmons. And then Kristen, whom I'd never met, copied all those pages for me and entered them into a website. I'll be eternally grateful.

Dixie Kline, for the good reads, constant encouragement, and help with the pictures.

Janice Ray Mayhew, for the assistance in telling Jawana's story about their nursing school days. She was certainly an invaluable help, even in remembering the make and color of car Jawana drove. But, as hard as she tried, she couldn't come up with the name of the Siamese cat.

Bill Scarbrough, for being my first interviewee and reader of the book as it was being written. He helped a lot.

Mark Gentry, for assisting me in the telling of the painful accounts of his brother's murder. I know it was hard, and I appreciate it.

Jewel Morris, Jr. and Jane Bowers, for a wonderful lunch and most helpful information.

Jim Martin, for building me a website I love. You're a genius.

Christina Scherrey, for being my little Whippersnapper.

Jr. Saulsberry, for the help with Baldor information.

Beverly Powell Bender, for your powerful recollections in helping me flesh out the characters.

Crawford County Sheriff Ron Brown, for pointing me in the right direction.

Jan at the Prosecuting Attorney's Office in Van Buren, for helping me with all three books.

Joan and Marty at the Now & Then Shoppe in Fort Smith, for the information about Holly Gentry. And thanks for helping me dress like a real writer.

Paula at Crabtree Farms, for all the good tomatoes and offering to drive me to the bare ground where the murders took place. Seeing the wide expanse of fertile land that once belonged to Clyde McClure, but was now the Crabtree Farm, gave me insight into just how lonely that land must have seemed on that January night of 1981.

Daniel Shue, for your encouragement and help.

Randy Smith, for your encouraging words and help concerning the courthouse in Van Buren, the town you love better than anyone I know.

Calline Ellis, for your memories of Jawana Price in nursing school.

Nellie DeWitt Oliver, for your friendship for over sixty years and your remembrances of Kibler and the folks who lived there.

Mary Jane Mustard, for the Kibler trips. You're a lot of fun to travel with down dirt roads. And you love books.

Eleanor Clark, for being my oldest and dearest friend.

Duke, Kimberly, and Meg at Pen-L Publishing, thanks for granting this old gal her chance to tell some pretty good stories.

And, most of all, to all the kind readers who joined my tribe. Thank you, thank you, thank you.

ABOUT THE AUTHOR

I've been around books all my life. My first job was working at the library at a sanatorium for people with TB. My last job was as a branch manager for the Fort Smith Public Library. In-between those first and last jobs, I taught school and worked in a bookstore. I feel a great comfort just by looking at my books in my shelves on either side of my living room fireplace.

Now I'm a true crime writer. Some have teased me and called me the Grandma Moses of True Crime. And with this third book, Cold Blooded, which will be published in my seventy-eighth year of life, I qualify for that esteemed title granted to me.

All my books are about murders committed in and around my home town of Van Buren, Arkansas. In all those cases, I had some connection with the victims, and sometimes with those who were convicted for the crimes. I try to tell my stories as if I was sitting at a kitchen table with a friend.

I'm grateful to those who buy my books, and especially to those who stand in line for an autograph. I hope you'll keep them on your bookshelves at home and find comfort just by looking at them.

Visit Anita at:
www.AnitaPaddock.com

Made in the USA
Coppell, TX
05 October 2020

Find more great reads at
Pen-L.com

Made in the USA
Monee, IL
10 June 2021